Europe and the Superpowers

Westview Replica Editions

The concept of Westview Replica Editions is a response to the continuing crisis in academic and informational publishing. Library budgets for books have been severely curtailed. Ever larger portions of general library budgets are being diverted from the purchase of books and used for data banks, computers, micromedia, and other methods of information retrieval. Interlibrary loan structures further reduce the edition sizes required to satisfy the needs of the scholarly community. Economic pressures on the university presses and the few private scholarly publishing companies have severely limited the capacity of the industry to properly serve the academic and research communities. As a result, many manuscripts dealing with important subjects, often representing the highest level of scholarship, are no longer economically viable publishing projects--or, if accepted for publication, are typically subject to lead times ranging from one to three years.

Westview Replica Editions are our practical solution to the problem. We accept a manuscript in camera-ready form, typed according to our specifications, and move it immediately into the production process. As always, the selection criteria include the importance of the subject, the work's contribution to scholarship, and its insight, originality of thought, and excellence of exposition. The responsibility for editing and proofreading lies with the author or sponsoring institution. We prepare chapter headings and display pages, file for copyright, and obtain Library of Congress Cataloging in Publication Data. A detailed manual contains simple instructions for preparing the final typescript, and our editorial staff is always available to answer questions.

The end result is a book printed on acid-free paper and bound in sturdy library-quality soft covers. We manufacture these books ourselves using equipment that does not require a lengthy make-ready process and that allows us to publish first editions of 300 to 600 copies and to reprint even smaller quantities as needed. Thus, we can produce Replica Editions quickly and can keep even very specialized books in print as long as there is a demand for them.

About the Book and Editors

Relations between the superpowers and the nations of Eastern and Western Europe are especially tenuous as the midpoint of the 1980s approaches. The contributors to this volume assess the current political, economic, and military dimensions of Europe's international relations and consider the prospects for change, focusing on the role of the rival alliance systems (NATO and the Warsaw Pact), Soviet conceptions of the future of Europe, U.S. goals concerning the maintenance of NATO, and Europe's assessment of its own interests and objectives. The book concludes by addressing the impact of Soviet and East European domestic developments on present and future East-West relations.

Steven Bethlen is the director of the Academy for Politics and Current Events of the Hanns-Seidel Foundation in Munich. His publications include *Osthandel in der Krise*. Ivan Volgyes is a professor of political science at the University of Nebraska. His publications include *Hungary: A Nation of Contradictions* (Westview).

Europe and the Superpowers

Political, Economic, and Military Policies in the 1980s

edited by Steven Bethlen
and Ivan Volgyes

Westview Press / Boulder and London

A Westview Replica Edition

Copyright © 1985 by Westview Press, Inc.

Published in 1985 in the United States of America by Westview Press, Inc., 5500 Central Avenue, Boulder, Colorado 80301; Frederick A. Praeger, Publisher

Library of Congress Cataloging in Publication Data
Europe and the superpowers.
    (A Westview replica edition)
    Bibliography: p.
    Includes index.
    1. Europe--National security--Addresses, essays, lectures. 2. North Atlantic Treaty Organization--Addresses, essays, lectures. 3. Warsaw Treaty Organization--Addresses, essays, lectures. 4. United States--Military relations--Europe--Addresses, essays, lectures.
5. Soviet Union--Military relations--Europe--Addresses, essays, lectures. 6. Europe--Military relations--United States--Addresses, essays, lectures. 7. Europe--Military relations--Soviet Union--Addresses, essays, lectures.
I. Bethlen, Stefan, Graf, 1946-   . II. Volgyes, Ivan, 1936-   .
UA646.E923 1985   355'.03304   84-19600
ISBN 0-86531-887-5

Printed and bound in the United States of America

10 9 8 7 6 5 4 3 2 1

Contents

viii

Foreword

As far as the prospects for peace and prosperity in the world were concerned, the decade of the 1980s did not augur well. In the US an American president came to power with the avowed program of challenging Soviet expansionism. In the Soviet Union, a sick and weak First Secretary was hampered by age and disease, inactive and incapable of decisive moves. In Western Europe, stormy electioneering reached heights of bitterness between conservatives and liberals, threatening fragile domestic political balances. And in Eastern Europe, the Polish malaise threatened to dismantle a bankrupt economic system teetering at the edge of disaster.

Nor did the military sphere provide a much better perspective for the combattants of East and West. The United States just began a large-scale modernization campaign to catch up with the advantages the USSR gained during the previous decade. The Soviet Union was going ahead with the deployment of medium-range missiles targeted at Western Europe, in spite of being bogged down in Afghanistan without seeing "a light at the end of the tunnel" of military involvement there. The forces of NATO were planning to increase their expenditures for the defense of the alliance system both on the battle-field and in technical areas, increases the Soviets could not expect readily to meet. And the Warsaw Pact, as usual, looked to the USSR for a decisive role to play in foreign military policy.

The crux of these conflicts, of course, was the competition between the United States and the USSR, the two true superpowers of the world, for exertion of their influence in Europe. While it was also a competition between the two systems, that of communism and liberal democracy, the contest between the superpowers was directed specifically at the maintenance of the spheres of influence that were determined during the various peace conferences of 1943-45. Although both superpowers were hopeful that the "other parts" of Europe would come under their influence -- and while both sides were wooing Europe and the Europeans -- neither power would be willing to risk an all-out war for accomplishing such a venture, realizing the risks of thermonuclear disaster that could possibly result from truly adventurous policies.

Unrecognized by both powers for quite a while was the fact, however, that during the past three-to-four decades since the end of World War II Europe -- if such an entity still can be spoken of -- has "grown up." It has come to maturity of a kind it has not known during the heights of colonial days; a maturity that came from the realization that, while these powers were no longer the superpowers of the present, they have interests that are separate and distinct from those of their respective alliances. And while, indeed, many of these interests were the same as those of the major superpowers which their major ties were maintained, there were other interests that were disparate from those of the US or the USSR.

To be sure, major differences also could be noted in the very nature of alliances and polities that existed in the East and West. In the East, the Warsaw Pact was imposed upon the nations of Eastern Europe and no state could unilaterally oppose the wishes of the Soviet Union, at least not in theory. But here, too, there were countries that failed to meet Soviet desiderata, for instance, in increasing the military expenditures desired by the Soviet Union; for various reasons, Romania, Hungary and Poland failed to allocate the amount the Soviet Union wished them to devote to defense. And while, of course, the people of Eastern Europe could not openly express their opposition to the "fraternal alliance," there were signs of non-official peace movements in East Germany, Czechoslovakia and even Hungary, and their activities displeased the local Communist elites to a great extent.

The situation was even more complex in Western Europe. Although during the subsequent elections, the Western European electorates have returned to power solid majorities of those who opposed the policies of the USSR and supported those of the new president of the US, there were sizable minorities that opposed American policies and those of the NATO alliance; although not necessarily supporting the policies of the USSR, those who opposed especially the defense policies of NATO, inter alia served notice to the world that they desired the adoptation of a policy that was unequivocally "neutralist" in the struggle between the superpowers.

It is, thus, against this background that the idea for this book was born in discussions between Stefan Graf Bethlen, the president of the Akademie für Politik und Zeitgeschehen of the Hanns Seidel Stiftung, and myself in June, 1982. We decided that using the format of the German-American Conference organized by the Hanns Seidel Stiftung, a group of distinguished European,

American and German scholars would try to pull together
some of these thoughts on superpower relations and
Europe. Under the auspices of the Stiftung, and with its
support, the conference was organized around two working
themes: "Osthandel in den 80'er Jahren" and "The
Superpowers and Europe." The group met at Wildbad
Kreuth, not far from Munich, on June 26-29, 1984 to
exchange the various perspectives, agreements and
disagreements the participants possessed regarding these
major and lasting problems. Under the chairmanship of
Stefan Graf Bethlen, Dr. Klaus Lange and myself, the
conference invited the following individuals to present
their views:

Pierre Hassner, Institut d'Etudes Politiques, Paris
William Griffith, Massachussetts Institute of
    Technology
A. Ross Johnson, The Rand Corporation
Jürgen Notzold, Stiftung Wissenschaft und Politik
Hermann Weber, Universität Hamburg
Peter Knirsch, University of Berlin
Vernon V. Aspaturian, Pennsylvania State University
Alfred Schueller, University of Marburg
Wolfram Hanrieder, University of California,
    Santa Barbara
George Schopflin, London School of Economics
Trond Gilberg, U.S. Army War College
John M. Montias, Yale University
Angela Stent, Georgetown University
William Saffran, University of Colorado
Ivan Volgyes, University of Nebraska
Robert C. Tucker, Princeton University
Paul Lendvai, University of Viennal and ORF
Katherine Kelleher, University of Maryland
Stephen Larrabee, Institute for East West Security
    Studies
William Reichert, Brown Brothers

The papers presented at the conference are contained
in updated form in the pages of this volume. The
analysts contributing these articles possess values
about politics and policies that are disparate. They do
not share a common "ideology," but they do share a
common belief in the necessity of open discussion,
pluralism of opinion, and commitments to the principles
of liberal democracy. And while the specialists writing
these articles may express differences in perspectives
and policy-ascriptions, those present at the meeting all
agreed that the most important task facing both European
and American scholars is to be open-minded and sensitive
to the perspectives of the policy-makers guiding the
various nations of the alliance system, and of the
people of these polities. For without an informed
public, our greatest achievement, the system of

stability and political democracy that has flowered for
the last three-to-four decades in Europe and the US, may
very well be threatened.

Ivan Volgyes
Lincoln, Nebraska
November 1983

Acknowledgments

The editors of this volume gratefully acknowledge the assistance of Mrs. Elsie Thomas and Mr. Gordon Anderson for their efforts in translating some of the studies appearing in this volume from German to English. Thanks are also due to Ms. Laura Holmgren of the University of Nebraska for able secretarial and editorial assistance.

1. Europe and the Superpowers: An Analytical Framework

George Schopflin

The Scope of the Problem

The concept of "Europe" has been regularly adopted and appropriated by a variety of political, social, cultural or economic groups and movements, with the result that the meaning of the concept has become decidedly vague. Furthermore, Europe can actually be defined by a variety of criteria -- geographical, linguistic, or for that matter, gastronomic. All of these definitions have their validity in one or another specific contexts. In this paper, however, the definition of Europe will be attempted from a different standpoint. The emphasis of this definition is on the politico-cultural roots which have produced the entity and the attidudinal matrix customarily called Europe. Inevitably, this involves certain ambiguities. It includes both subjective attitudes and beliefs, but equally a number of shared historical experiences. In particular, the definition may be blurred at the edges -- there are doubtful cases in both time and place -- but at the end of the day, this does not alter the validity of the central core argument. In essence, the definition of Europe adopted here constitutes a kind of mental map of factors, events and perceptions with politically significant consequences.

At the heart of the definition is a set of shared experiences. These have been an interaction of political, economic and above all cultural processes. What differentiates Europe from other great politico-cultural areas, like China or Mesopotamia or India is the particular pattern of these shared experiences and the way in which they were incorporated in the consciousness of European history. Thus the European experience included the era of medieval universalism, the Renaissance, the Reformation and Counter-Reformation, the Enlightenment and the Era of Nationalism. Individual non-European or semi-European units may have shared in one or another of these experiences. Thus while China underwent an entirely different historical

experience from Europe, the Chinese political tradition
did include a certain concept of political reciprocity
and a limited acceptance of the market. Japan developed
institutions with some resemblance to European
feudalism. What differentiated Europe and ensured its
uniqueness is having experienced one particular set of
historical processes in a linear and causally linked
pattern. The causal link is crucial for this definition.
It is assumed as axiomatic that, for example, the
Reformation would not have come about without a decay in
Catholic universalism or that the origins of Romantic
Nationalism must be sought in the Age of Enlightenment.
It is noteworthy that these various processes may have
been experienced in different forms and at different
levels of intensity by the various parts of Europe, but
these variations remained within a single, overall
framework. Those parts of the world that did not undergo
this particular pattern, therefore, are on this
definition outside Europe.

The Political Tradition

The separateness and specificity of the European
tradition is most evident in the political realm. The
crucial European contribution to the technology of
government has been the insistence on the division of
power and the division of the legitimation of power. In
the European tradition, power is not to be the monopoly
possession of the ruler and likewise legitimation is not
merged with power itself but subject to external
constraints. Clearly, where the ruler does not control
his own legitimation, he is subject potentially to
delegitimation and hence cannot be regarded as absolute.
Traditionally in Europe, the division was between
religious and temporal power, a phenomenon that was
acted out most strikingly in the political drama of
Canossa. But this fragmentation of power had other
aspects. In particular, the feudal system recognized a
reciprocity of rights and obligations and, equally
importantly, an autonomous system of courts to enforce
these. This can be regarded as the original impulse for
the insistence upon a mutuality of obligations between
ruler and ruled. In international organization and
relations, Europe developed the competitive state, the
idea that no one state -- an imperium -- should dominate
the entire politico-cultural area, despite the legacy
of empire from Rome and the attempt by the Holy Roman
Empire to act as its heir. This again is quite different
from the state systems developed elsewhere, like the
imperial entities in Mesopotamia or the Chinese empire.
In the economy, the diversity and variety of Europe, as
well as its rapid and intensive growth, rested on the
concept of the market. Despite hostility at various
times to uncontrolled economic activity and the power

derived from capital accumulation, neither the church nor secular rulers were able to curb the market. This failure to curtail the freedom of economic initiative became the foundation of the particular pattern of an unfettered exchange of goods and ideas that have been central to European development. The role of towns as autonomous centers of interaction and as centers of specializations in a variety of fields independent of the ruler can hardly be overemphasized. These gave rise to the growth of new technologies, especially in the area of banking. The existence of effective networks of communication and transport covering the entire cultural area provided for continuous, high level exchanges, thereby promoting borrowing and exchanges of ideas and goods and ultimately a certain sense of community. In this way, the variety of Europe has been held within a single, broad cultural framework. Finally, the role of urban centers has been pivotal in the evolution of competing political identities, which eventually played a key role in the process of modernization. The constant challenge and scrutiny prevented stagnation and encouraged change.

<u>Political</u> <u>Modernization</u>
The phenomenon of accelerating change and the limits on the power of the ruler can be said to have given rise to what is termed "modernity." At the center of this much contested concept are change, complexity and choice. There is a half-explicit imperative that as societies change, their members should have an ever-wider range of choice over their political futures. In traditional, static systems, state-society relations are largely within the power of the ruler; the ruler has control of the political agenda; and the interests of the individuals and groups are subsumed in the will of the ruler. Traditional societies can achieve considerable stability on this basis. Once the process of modernity has begun to erode these props of the traditional ruler, all aspects of his power come under scrutiny and have to be justified according to the new criteria encapsulated in the slogan of the French Revolution. The exceptional access to politics on the basis of, say, birth can no longer be justified under the new conditions. In socio-economic terms, the expansion and extension of political rights has been accompanied and intensified by the rise of the mass market and large-scale technology, which have helped to transform the traditional <u>gemeinschaft</u> into the modern <u>gesellschaft</u>.
Thus at the center of modernity has been the redefinition of the European tradition of the interplay between ruler and ruled, between state and society. The model that emerged in the 19th century accepted a

considerable degree of control by society over political power and placed emphasis on the continuation of modernization through individual initiative and the aggregation of conflicts of interest through the market. At the same time, the traditional European repugnance towards the concentration of power found its expression in the strict separation of political and economic power (in the doctrine of laissez faire) and in the division of political and economic legitimation. The slow movement towards the fusion of these two has been one of the features of the 20th century.

It is noteworthy that this is not the only model of modernity possible or conceivable. The traditional Russian concept, in accordance with the prevailing preference for the concentration rather than the division of power, has involved modernization from above. This is a perfectly viable model. To take a contrasting pair of examples: in the United States, the West was opened up by individual action with minimal state participation, whereas Siberia was opened up as the conscious and deliberate action of the Russian state. Both can be regarded as successful in their own terms.

Whereas in the 19th century, modernization was pushed forward overwhelmingly by autonomous action from below with the state playing the role of "night watchman," in the 20th century these roles have been reversed. The state now plays a far more active part in determining the political agenda, in launching economic initiatives and in providing an activist regulatory framework for society. In this sense, the traditional etatist values of the European past, the respect invested in the ruler, reemerged in a modern form under the impact of the dislocation attendant on modernization. Particularly noteworthy was the mounting cost of technology, especially military technology, to levels where only the state could underwrite it. This inevitably resulted in a far more interventionist state than existed in the 19th century. However, the state of affairs in Western Europe has not produced a complete overlordship of state over society. Although the state is preeminent, it remains to some extent under the control of society. Hence the contemporary political order depends neither purely on the market nor purely on state control, but is a mixture of the two. In this sense, there is no capitalism in Europe, but a system which should be termed etatist with market elements. A great deal of activity continues to be regulated by the market -- politically as well as economically -- but much is now accepted as being within the ambit of state responsibility. Where the line should be drawn has, in effect, been the subject of a continuous debate in Europe since 1945. The reemergence of the questioning of the overextended role of the state has produced

5

governments claiming that their mission is to push back the frontiers of the state; their record in the early 1980s suggested that this was much easier at the level of rhetoric than in practice.

The Socialist Alternative

One of the crucial shared experiences of Europe, although it has seldom been perceived in this way, has been socialism. Socialism, naturally, has attracted numerous definitions, but for present purposes, the Socialist "project" will be defined as the following: a.) the extensions of all political and corresponding socio-economic rights on an equal basis to all members of the political community; and b.) the recreation of the gemeinschaft under conditions of modernity. The fact that socialism in all its forms has to date failed in both these challenges is, for present purposes, immaterial. More significant is that the whole of Europe has had experience of the socialist vision, has absorbed it into its ideal image of the world and continues to order its sense of the future by it. Hence the failures of socialism as practised are likewise irrelevant, because it is an ideal type of society by which contemporary solutions are assessed. It is probably no exaggeration to say that for many, if not most, Europeans futurity and progress are perceived at some level in terms that are recognizably within the socialist frame of reference. All this is in spite of the unsatisfactory results of the Socialist types of systems which Europe has actually experienced. In particular, the substitution of the state for gemeinschaft by the creation of social welfare safety nets has seen a burgeoning of bureaucratic intervention in the life of society without any countervailing control mechanism. Furthermore, much of the original socialist vision of freedom and individual autonomy has been conflated with a pre-modern anti-capitalism and conservatism, with the result of strengthening etatist trends.

Europe and the Superpowers

Europe's relations with the superpowers have been complex and varied. If the 19th century was a period of European preeminence and even dominance, the 20th century has seen a shrinking of Europe and a quest for redefinition outwards as well as internally. Arguably, both Russia and the United States have had a long and involved relationship with Europe. For Europe, Russia was traditionally a peripheral power of some significance, a competitor for land and, in the 19th century, an active participant in the European system. Yet despite a veneer of Europeanness at this time, the Russian political and cultural tradition was always very different, something which was sometimes fully

appreciated and sometimes not. This acquisition of
European qualities by Russia came to an abrupt halt in
1917 and thereafter European perceptions of the Soviet
Union tended to be marked by very different
considerations of fear and, on the part of some,
sympathy for its socialist goals. In any case, Europe
was obliged by force of circumstances to reconsider its
role in the world after the Great European Civil War of
1914-1945, which left it weakened and dependent on the
superpowers. After 1945, Europe embarked on a process of
stabilizing itself internally and of accepting a
diminished role in a new world order the agenda of which
was set by others. The redefinition of Europe in
relation to the Soviet Union proved to be relatively
straightforward. The Bolshevik Revolution pulled Russia
onto an entirely new path, which had little in common
with the traditions evolved in Europe, and, indeed,
despite the socialist language in which the character of
the USSR was clothed, it proved to be little more than
the recreation of a Russian tradition of accelerated
modernization imposed from above. The rejection of
European values, like the division of power and the
acceptance of some control over the state by society,
left the two parties as far apart as they could be. The
weakening of Europe after 1945 only intensified the fear
of the superpower in the East.

On the other hand, differentiation vis-à-vis the
United States has been nothing like as simple. Europe
shares much, though far from all, with the US and
definitions of interest have been complex and sometimes
painful. This area of self-definition, in contrast to
and at times against the US has been a key feature of
the slow emergence of a European identity in the
post-1945 period. The problems raised by this have been
many and they are often highly complex, so much so that
distinctions are decidedly blurred at the edges. By
comparison with the US, Europe tends to be more attached
to tradition and to be more cautious about innovation;
the role accorded to the state is accepted as wider and
more powerful; by the same token, society in Europe
generally accepts that it has a less salient role than
in the United States; and, in the current period at
least, Europeans are less receptive to change and
innovation than is the norm in the US, but it may be
that once the long trauma of the 1914-1945 era has
disappeared, this will change. Even in the 19th century,
when much of what one associates with the American
tradition was formulated and when, given the comparative
weakness of the state in Europe at the time, the two
resembled each other most closely, there were already
distinct patterns in deference to authority, class
structures and the setting of the agenda for change. The
rhetoric of populist language and the apparent readiness
in America to couch political discourse in what appears

to Europeans as hyperbole confuses and concerns many
Europeans -- a confusion that is particularly notable in
the United Kingdom where it is intensified by the
sharing of variants of the same language. These
differences between Europe and America were intensified
by the 20th century, when the US did not share in the
European Civil War and the trauma of Europe after 1945.
European decolonization enhanced the trauma and was,
again, not shared by the US; the emergence of a distinct
European view of the world was further ensured by the
perception that decolonization was rushed through at the
behest of the US -- Suez was a particularly painful
experience for the two largest colonial states -- and by
the fact that decolonization was accompanied by the new
world order mostly created according to American codes
of behavior and ideals. With the inevitable shrinking of
European horizons, relations with the superpowers moved
into a separate sphere, from which Europe was partially
excluded, even when European interests were involved. In
all these respects, therefore, a distinctively
articulated European interest, in competition with that
of the US, has arisen and has acted to offset the wide
range of complimentarity between the two, even while
this contest has undoubtedly helped the evolution of a
European identity.

The European Periphery

The place of Central and Eastern Europe in the
longue durée of European patterns has been on the
periphery. Eastern Europe has shared in some, but not
all of the experiences of Europe and often with a much
diminished intensity. Thus society never developed the
same political muscle; the principle of reciprocity was
weak; the role of the state was always more prominent as
the principal agent of modernization; the area remained
economically backward by comparison; and the political
tradition of the periphery tended to accept a much
higher degree of authoritarianism than the center.
Nonetheless by many criteria, especially cultural,
Eastern Europe can be counted a part of the all-European
area and this is demonstrated not least by the
persistent difficulties experienced with the forcibly
imposed alien system of governance that has obtained
there since the Communist revolution. The area will be
plagued with weakness and instability until this
decorrelation is overcome. Not that the dominant
superpower is likely to countenance this in the near
future. The three post-Communist takeover attempts to
transform the Soviet-type systems of the area were each
met by firm rebuffs. It is also noteworthy that there
was a progressive increase in West European
identification with these East European experiments. The
Hungarian Revolution was written off as an unfortunate
excess on the part of the Hungarians; the Prague Spring

attracted considerably more West European attention, not
least because the Czechoslovak leaders openly proclaimed
their intention of "Europeanizing" their political
system; and the values of democracy and autonomy were,
inter alia, very highly acclaimed during the Solidarity
era in Poland. If there was, at the same time, a measure
of misunderstanding of what was actually happening in
Eastern Europe at these points, that should not detract
from the underlying sense of shared identity, however
loosely defined, between Eastern and Western Europe and,
by definition, implicitly feeling that Soviet control
over this area was in some way unacceptable.

A European Identity

The question must finally be posed, what actually
constitutes a European identity today and what interests
are specifically European? While in practice, these are
often defined by the needs of day-to-day political
decision making, there are some broad underlying
patterns, derived from the antecedent processes
described above. In the first place, there is a
commitment to democratic government that rests on a
balance between the interests of the individual and
those of the community, with much (though not all) of
this being defined by the state. Second, there is a
readiness to identify the community with the state and
to use the instruments of the state for the resolution
of conflicts on a broad front in preference to
regulation by society. Third, there is an understanding
that change is welcome, but that it should not
constitute too radical a break with the past; continuity
has a major role to play and revolutions do not. Fourth,
the strength of Europe has been to combine diversity
with a broad cultural unity, within which agreement and
disagreement have been about the same subject matter.
And last, there is a barely perceptible sense that
Europe extends beyond its present scope geopolitically
and includes or should include Eastern Europe within its
zone of cultural radiation. The solution of this,
however, is a matter of the longest possible term.

2. Western Europe and the United States: Reciprocal Diffusion, Convergence, and the Prospects of a Non-Military Atlanticism

William Safran

The Uncertainties of Military Atlanticism

There is the story of a Turkish sea captain who brings a shipment of several tons of sardines into the Greek harbor at Piraeus. He meets an Italian merchant, and offers him the shipment at the bargain price of $100. The Italian soon resells the shipment to a Frenchman at the bargain rate of $200; the latter, in turn, sells it to a Belgian for $300. The shipment continues to change hands until, finally, an American businessman sells the sardines to a German for $1000. After the transaction the German gets hungry, goes to his hotel room, and opens one of the cans of sardines. But when he begins to eat, he realizes the sardines are rotten. Indignantly, he complains to the American who replies: "You fool, these sardines are not for eating -- they are for buying and selling!"

For the past several years, discussions in Western Europe and the United States about the relationship between these two regions has focused around the question of the current state and relevance of the Atlantic alliance. There are those who have questioned whether NATO, as the dominant expression of that alliance, is still meaningful, in view of the loss of nuclear monopoly by the United States. Since the willingness of the United States to use its strategic nuclear weapons in the defense of Europe -- and expose American cities to the risk of destruction in Soviet counterstrikes -- is uncertain, the NATO conventional forces are inadequate, and the Europeans' attitudes about the place of tactical nuclear weapons are ambivalent, much of the argument about the utility of stockpiles, firepower, costs, and deterrent force is like the argument about the sardines: they can be bargained for and sold, but when used may have a harmful and perhaps fatal effect on the user.

To many American politicians and military leaders, the fact that Western Europe has not been invaded by the USSR in the past generation constitutes sufficient proof of the effectiveness of NATO; but to others, NATO rests

10

on promises that have not been kept, lies that have
begun to be exposed, pretenses that are gradually being
uncovered, and assumptions that have not proven tenable.
According to one observer[1], NATO was based on "the
illusion that the Alliance would lead to a true
partnership of equals with virtually identical
interests." According to another[2], German adherence to
NATO -- a most crucial element -- was based on a lie:
the premise, no matter how implicit, of unification.
Recently, one scholar[3] has argued that the purely
military definition of NATO is inadequate, and that "the
NATO plant must grow or wither"; while to another[4], the
alliance has become "an empty shell."

Official American decision-makers cannot, of course,
publicly agree with such assessments. Alexander Haig,
while still US Secretary of State, followed his
predecessors in asserting that NATO would remain because
it is the expression of a number of commonalities
subsumed under the rubric of "Atlantic civilization." As
Haig put it:

"The alliance survives...because the Atlantic family
of nations is inspired by a common faith in the
capacity of all men for self-government... As free
peoples, we obey the laws passed by governments we
have freely chosen. Our military forces take orders
from elected civilian authority...The Atlantic
nations constitute an enduring natural community
with many economic, and organizational links beside
NATO itself."

Such rhetoric may be questioned, especially in view
of the fact that for many years after the establishment
of NATO nondemocratic regimes continued to exist in
Spain, Portugal, Greece and Turkey. But it has been
argued that the NATO military machinery, with its
hundreds of committees, liason offices, and specialized
agencies -- even if not used, or not capable of being
used, for real-life military purposes -- by their very
existence help to foster a broadly based Atlantic
consciousness that must spill over into a non-military
Atlanticism. In fact, this "neofunctionalist"
expectation is explicit in the original NATO treaty
itself. The preamble refers to common political values,
and Article 2 proclaims the intention of the signatories
to "the strengthening of free institutions... the
promotion of conditions of stability and well-being...
and the elimination of conflict in their international
economic policies."

As we know, such hopes have not been fully met,
owing to a number of circumstances. The most widely
cited has been the lack of diplomatic solidarity within
the NATO camp, for which blame must be apportioned both
to the USA and the West European countries. During the

Franco-Algerian war, the USA ignored the feelings of the French when it failed to support them, both on the battlefield and in the United Nations; during the Suez crisis, the USA collaborated with the USSR against the British and French; and the Vietnam war was pursued by the USA against the disapproval of the major European nations. European countries, for their part, were half-hearted in their criticisms of Soviet behavior in Afghanistan and Poland; during the various Arab-Israeli wars, while the USA's attitudes ranged from pro-Israel to neutral, those of most Western European countries ranged from neutrality to hostility to the Jewish state. These differences, of course, had to do with the fact that the existence of the Atlantic community did not negate narrower national interests. It is unclear whether these interests were capable of being pursued because NATO was a success in that it provided an effective umbrella over the West European countries and gave them a certain playroom; whether, on the contrary, NATO was perceived to be militarily so useless as to require the West European nations to look out for themselves and make their own accommodations with the USSR; or whether the Soviet threat had receded to the extent of making the Atlantic Alliance irrelevant.

It is pointless to argue whether the national policies of the USA were more irrational, or more destructive of Atlantic unity, than those of selected European countries. In view of its global responsibilities and its bipolar, or Manichean, view of world politics, the USA is bound to dismiss European national concerns as too parochial, and even as "atavistic."[6] For their part, Western Europeans have criticized American policies for a number of reasons: if these policies concern Latin America, they are indicative of an old-fashioned economic imperialism; if they concern the Middle East, they take insufficient account of the vital economic interests of European countries. Beyond these specific matters, there has always been a general, perhaps "generic," European distrust of American foreign policy, and of the motivations that have inspired it. Much of this distrust is related to a resentment of the American superpower status. For many generations, West European nations had been the chief movers and shakers of global policy -- not only because of their relative economic power and their colonial possessions but also becasue of the dynastic interconnections of their rulers and the polyglot finesse of their diplomats. Today it is the USA that has the raw military and economic power, but it does not use that power properly. The USA is often viewed as a naive if not slightly barbaric giant whose money has not been a substitute for maturity and whose diplomats have been moving on the global stage with feet of clay. While the USA often chooses not to use its raw power on a large scale -- and often uses it

for the promotion of the short-term interests of
prominent economic sectors (i.e., the profits of large
corporations) -- the Europeans have tried to parlay
their powerlessness into authority and influence: either
by acting as if they had raw power, or by pretending to
a superior intellectual or moral position. Of course,
this exercise of European power has been largely
symbolic: the bursts of indignation coming from European
countries -- at first mostly from Gaullist France but
increasingly from West Germany as well -- regarding the
misguided American policies in the Middle Esat, Central
America, and Southeast Asia have affected these
policies, or the global constellation of power, as
little as has the glittering presence of European
statesmen at international conferences in Paris, London,
or Rome.

Cognitive Dissonances and Demonologies
     For many years following World War II, the
giganticism of the USA was accepted and even admired:
Americans were viewed as generous, reasonable, modest
and "innocent," while the Russians were seen as
dogmatic, rigid, and aggressive. Now there has been a
partial reversal of roles: the Russians are no longer
feared, while the Americans are disliked -- or, to put
it more accurately, the Russians are disliked less than
the Americans. This is particularly the case in West
Germany, which used to be considered the arch-
atlanticist in Europe because it hated the Bolsheviks
more than did other Western European countries. This
change of attitude is reflected in the relatively muted
West German criticism of the crackdown in Poland and,
more recently, the rise of the Greens.
     There are several reasons for the "destigmatization"
of the USSR and the parallel "demonization" of the USA.
There is, first, the matter of pure economic opportunism: the prospects of lucrative trade with the USSR
makes Western Europeans appreciative of the business-
like, non-ideological behavior of Soviet trading
officials, which is seen to contrast with the tendency
of American diplomats in Western Europe to moralize
about freedom and democracy. Related to this, there is
the economic rivalry with the USA, and the resentment of
American hypocrisy -- the most recent example being the
Americans criticizing the European pipeline agreement
with the USSR while they themselves were arranging to
sell grain to the USSR.
     Second, there is the traditional cultural contempt
of the European elite for the USA -- whether justified
or not -- which is fortified by the persistent presence
of the American diplomat who knows only English and who,
while in Europe, prefers to stay in an American enclave.
This contempt is strengthened by the image of an inept
American leadership, an image that manifested itself in

13

the summer of 1981, when the American vice-president, while on a visit to Paris, publicly criticized President Mitterrand's decision to include four Communists in the government; and that is fed by the frequent refusal (or perhaps inability) of American politicians to differentiate between Communists and Socialists. The contempt for the quality of American leadership inevitably translates into a mystification over the entire American political system that can produce such leaders -- and over the American failure to bring its institutions up to date.

Thirdly, there is the fact that the USA and Western Europe view the Soviet Union quite differently. Americans tend to see the USSR as a functional conglomerate held together by power and ideology and determined to destabilize and subjugate much of the rest of the world, while Western Europeans (and not only Gaullists) take into account the persistent reality of Russia and its cultural dimensions and with its historical ties to Europe.

To some extent, the American view of the Soviet Union was paralleled by a widely held Western European view of the USA. European intellectuals have been unwilling to grant a truly "national" reality to the USA, preferring to think of it as a country without its own history or civilization. Conversely, Americans have tended to see Western Europe as a whole by ignoring the cultural and historic differences among the French, Germans, Italians, and others. This inability to see internal nuances has often caused Americans to view Western European nations much like the 13 original colonies -- that is, as components of a federal United States of Europe. And the same ignorance has made Americans more sanguine about the prospects of an Atlantic community.

The stigmatization of the USA by West Europeans can also be explained in concrete functional terms: anti-Americanism has served as a device for mobilizing several West European nations behind the effort at uniting Europe in the context of the European Economic Community (EEC). Furthermore, in France, it has been used as a weapon for transpartisan consensus building, especially under the Gaullists. For West Germany, anti-Americanism has served still another function: in their attempts to deal with their own past (Bewältigung der Vergangenheit) and to exculpate themselves for their behavior during the Nazi regime, Germans have "universalized" their guilt by pointing to deplorable behavior by others. And with the dimming of memories of cruel acts committed by Red Army soldiers more than three decades ago, it has served West German psychological needs to dwell on the persecution of Blacks in the USA, on the bombing of Hiroshima, and on the American cruelties in Vietnam and Central America.

In the interest of Atlantic unity, Americans have, by and large, not thrown their reproaches back; on the contrary, they have (particularly during the Eisenhower-Dulles years) been rather more "soft" toward West Germans than toward other West Europeans. The American favoritism toward West Germany, which has continued to cause Americans to view a special German-American relationship as the cornerstone of the Atlantic Alliance, must be attributed not so much to the location of West Germany at the frontlines of the great-power conflict in Europe as to the fact that for many years West Germany seemed to be developing an American-style "mechanistic" view of community, and hence to be more receptive to the idea of Atlanticism. To be more specific:

1. Like the USA, West Germany began as an artifact of politics, and constitutes a break with history: the USA had been established by breaking away from traditional monarchical patterns and by intending to be a new experiment; West Germany has a "half-nation" -- constituted a reversal of the national unification process that had begun more than a century earlier. Moreover, West Germany, by adhering to a federal tradition similar to that of the USA, would be a more understanding partner of the latter.

2. Compared to Britain and France, West Germany had little to lose, and much to gain, from an Atlantic embrace: with the end of World War II, its natural unity had been destroyed; to be German was an embarrassment; and a greater European regional structure, as a vehicle for facilitating a voluntary selbstentdeutschung, had not yet come into being.

3. By adopting a set of policies based on market economics, West Germany appeared to be an apt pupil of the USA; just as for many Americans "the business of America /was largely/ business," so for many Germans[9] the Bundesrepublik was essentially the Bundeswirtschaft.

4. Since West Germany had neither the national unity nor the nationalist ambitions of Gaullist France nor yet the global pretenses of Britain, it was the least troublesome, and therefore most comfortable, American ally.

The all-too-frequent articulation, by American leaders and political commentators, of the American enchantment with West Germany -- an activity occasionally[10] echoed by the British in their conflict with France -- proved to be somewhat counter-productive to Atlantic unity; to many Frenchmen, Belgians, Dutch and other Western Europeans of the older generation, who remembered the war and to whom the specter of a future West German revisionist policy -- another Rapallo -- was real, such a favoritism was a premature attempt to wipe out the distinction between

aggressor nations and their victims and to put West
Germany on the same political (and therefore moral)
level as the rest of the European countries.

One of the major problems facing the Atlantic
community (beyond a purely military arrangement) is, of
course, the existence of a number of countermodels, or
at least "countermagnets." One of these countermodels is
said to be the Communist world of the Soviet Union and
Eastern Europe -- as a logical consequence of the
"demonization" of the USA to which reference was made
above.

Several years ago, Zbigniew Brzezinski wrote an
article -- it must serve as an illustration of the
pitfalls of instant history -- arguing that there was a
crisis of society, ideology, and stability that was
leading Western Europe in the wrong, i.e., Eastward,
direction and hence boded ill for Atlantic unity. As
it turned out, the symptoms Brzezinski discovered were
either misperceived or not provably damaging to the
Euro-Atlantic relationship. Thus, the decline of
political stability that he detected from the "extreme
left parties" in France, Italy and Iberia was arrested
or reversed by the domestication of Communist parties in
Italy and Spain, and their decline, somewhat later, in
France and Portugal. He spoke of the "intensifying
radicalization of the intelligentsia" of Western Europe,
but failed to notice the growing popularity of
anti-Marxist thinking (even in France, as with the "new
philosophers") and of a technocratic and non-ideological
outlook within the old elite. Among other symptoms that
were detrimental to Atlantic unity were "new class and
ethnic cleavages." But the fact is that ethnic cleavages
-- which have resulted in large part from the mass
influx of foreign workers and refugees, and which are
still less serious in Europe than in the USA -- have had
the effect of reducing class cleavages, and of helping
to redefine European society in a more "American" (i.e.,
less "organicist" and more "functionalist") sense, and
hence of contributing to a Euro-Atlantic convergence.
Finally, he argued that because of the economic crisis
of the mid-1970s, many West Europeans viewed Eastern
European Communist systems with their "planned
development...the apparent absence of inflation and
economic cycles...and the presence of steady
employment..." as attractive counter-models "which could
at some point interact with latent resentment among many
West Europeans over the division of their continent into
two dependent parts, each to some extent modeling itself
on the social experience of its patron state." But in
the mid- and late 1970s, many West Europeans evinced a
reduced enthusiasm for planning, and turned more
sympathetically to "neo-liberal" policies. Moreover, the
economic mismanagement in the USSR, and the drastic

decline in industrial production and the growing food shortages in Poland, could not have escaped the notice of European intellectuals.

To be sure, there have been historic elements of a common European culture, and some of them continue to transcend East-West divisions. These include linguistic unities (as between East and West Germany), religious commonalities (e.g., Roman Catholicism, which is as strong in Poland as in Italy), and perhaps even -- despite more than a generation of Communist rule -- some similarities in the class systems. Other things that have united East and West Europe at one time or another have been occasional resentment of (West) Germany and fear of a possible resurgence of German power; a mutual awareness of client status; and a common opposition to American policies in Vietnam, Central America and the Middle East. (Anti-Israel positions on both sides of the Iron Curtain are to some extent based on anti-Semitism, which will continue to be a point de repère in the foreseeable future, irrespective of the number of Jews living in European countries.) But these commonalities will not suffice to produce "an alternative to partition" between East and West that certain scholars evoked during the heyday of optimism about détente. There is no indication that East-West convergence has been facilitated by the Helsinki agreements or by Ostpolitik. By contrast, there have been numerous developments that are indicative of a diffusion of institutions, policies, social patterns and cultural and economic products -- a diffusion that might be seen as leading to a Euro-Atlantic convergence that transcends a purely military Atlanticism.

Asymmetrical Diffusion

Diffusion may be defined as the spreading of ideas, institutions, socio-economic and cultural patterns, forms of behavior and attitudes from one country to another. The process may involve a variety of approaches and directions, and may imply any of the following:

1. A freely decided importation, on the basis of a rational examination of a variety of options and the conviction that the option chosen will work best;

2. The enforced adoption of an institution or pattern -- e.g., the adoption of Napoleonic laws in various European countries in the early 19th century; or the Sovietization of political and economic institutions in Eastern Europe after World War II;

3. The adoption of a foreign pattern for tactical or decorative purposes -- e.g., the opting for a republican government in Germany after World War II; the writing of a "federal" constitution by the Soviet Union in 1922; or the establishment of "parliaments" in Third-World countries;

4. Subtle suggestion, influence, or pressure -- e.g., informal pressures exerted by the Council of Europe on a number of West European countries to improve their substantive human-rights catalogues and their due-process provisions;
5. The harmonization of domestic laws or patterns with a transnational or supranational standard -- e.g., value-added taxes and social-security measures under the Common Market -- normally on the basis of treaties.

The importing of American-style things into Western Europe cannot always be clearly fitted into this or that typology of diffusion, especially since the term "Americanization" sometimes refers less to a deliberate copying than to the modernization of techniques, processes and patterns (often, but not always) pioneered in the USA.

For many years, the direction of diffusion was westward (with the possible exception of certain political ideas[12]). Although the founding of the United States constituted a deliberate break with the European political tradition, American legal and administrative patterns, educational curricula, language and culture -- and the maps of its immigrants -- were European; and, at least until the end of the 19th century, Europe remained the source of inspiration for American scientists, teachers, writers, artists, and dilettantes. After World War II, the direction of diffusion changed abruptly; Western European countries, in a burst of efforts to modernize their political socio-economic structures, imported a host of American things -- beyond supermarkets, highrise buildings, chewing gum, Coca-Cola, and the automobile culture. Among the more notable reforms are those relating to education: the democratization of educational structures, the "comprehensivization" of secondary schooling, the selective opening up of the university to the working class, the adaptation of the traditional classical-humanistic curriculum to the requirements of the modern job market by the addition of modern, science- and technology-oriented, subjects -- all these relied heavily on the American experience, although Western European reformers have sometimes been reluctant to admit this. In the realm of government and politics, there is little doubt that in instituting the practice of judicial review of legislation West Germany, Austria, Italy and (to a somewhat lesser extent) France were informed, and perhaps inspired, by the American prototype. The same is true of the interest -- in particular beginning in the late 1950s -- in the regionalization or administrative "deconcentration" experiments in several European countries with unitary systems. The transformation of the ideology-ridden multiparty systems into bipolar systems in which

concrete programs and personalities are important, e.g.,
in West Germany, Austria and France, is also a
manifestation of convergence with American (or
Anglo-American) patterns -- although this development
must in part be attributed to other factors as well: new
electoral methods, the decreasing relevance of old
ideologies in the face of social and economic changes,
and the "personalization" of political contests brought
about by television[13]
    Similar Americanization trends can be observed in
patterns of unionization and collective bargaining.
"Business unionism" now competes with ideological (e.g.,
anarcho-syndicalist, Catholic, or autogestionnaire)
unionism in France and Italy, and has more or less
displaced it in West Germany and Austria. Although in
some countries this development benefited from direct
assistance by the USA (the "AFL-CIA," as some Europeans
have suggested), it was in part a reflection of the
evolution of attitudes within Western Europe in favor of
more "autonomous bargaining" in the context of a
"liberal" (or American-style) definition of pluralism,
according to which unions and other voluntary
associations are on a par with, rather than inferior to,
the public authorities in terms of legitimacy.
    Several generalizations emerge from an analysis of
Euro-American diffusion: 1.) Few if any of these pattern
adaptations ("Americanizations") have been spillovers
from the complex military relationships and structures
of NATO; 2.) The importation of selected American
gadgets and patterns does not necessarily add up to
Atlantic civilization: the fact that Kentucky fried
chicken is eaten, Levis are worn, and English is widely
used, in Hong Kong, Taiwan, Israel, Panama, and even
parts of Eastern Europe does not make these regions part
of the Atlantic community; and 3.) There has not been an
equivalent "Europeanization" of the United Sates. Since
the end of World War II the USA has not, seemingly,
imported much more from Western Europe than war brides,
displaced persons, war criminals, wine-drinking habits,
pop music (The "Beatles"), perhaps new strains of
gonorrhea that are resistant to penicillin, and, more
recently, an interest in soccer. This is particularly
puzzling in view of the fact that, until the early
1970s, the number of Americans visiting Europe has been
infinitely greater than the number of Europeans visiting
the USA. But none of the major types of American
travelers to Europe -- the GIs, the government
officials, and the lower, middle and working classes on
packaged tours -- have been ideal carriers of culture.
The GIs and diplomats have tended to live in self-
contained American compounds, relatively insulated from
the "native" life around them; the ordinary American
tourist, while enjoying the famous sights, has probably

viewed European culture -- and therefore most things
European -- as too "high" or "quaint" to be suitable for
importation to the USA.
    Euro-Atlantic diffusion has been characterized not
only by a lack of symmetry and synchronism, but also by
an uneven impact. There is no doubt that
"Americanization" has affected the European masses,
whereas "Europeanization" has been largely confined to
the American elite. Thus it is the elite in the USA who
drink wine, eat French bread and soft cheese, and watch
European theater productions; and it is the American
intellectual who may learn European languages and
assimilate selected European ideologies -- often
somewhat belatedly. In the 1930s and 1940s, European
approaches to social analysis, historiography, literary
criticism, and philosophy (e.g. logical positivism, and
later, "critical theory") were absorbed by the American
academic establishment after they had been suppressed,
or lost their glitter, in Europe. Marxism (often under
the code label of "political economy") became popular in
many American universities in the mid-1970s, just when
it appeared to be going out of style in Western Europe;
similarly, there has been a growing recognition of the
autonomy of the state among American political
scientists (who may call themselves "structuralist"),
just when Western European social scientists
increasingly question the traditional sanctity of the
state.[14]

Elites and Elite Perceptions
    Some years ago, American scholars placed a great
deal of hope in the American and European elite, who
would be the vanguard in the effort at creating an
Atlantic community. It is not certain that this hope was
entirely justified. There are various elites, each with
its own perceptions, not all of which have reflected a
commitment to transnational convergence. The higher
administrative elite -- the civil servants of different
national governments -- is the least likely agent of
Euro-Atlanticism, since (if we exempt the "Eurocracy" in
Brussels) it has been oriented, by training and role,
toward the nation-state. The intellectual elite may show
a capacity for thinking in transnational and
universalistic terms; but in some countries (e.g.,
France), its humanistic component often thinks in terms
of cultural nationalism, while in others (e.g., the
USA), intellectuals have relatively little influence on
policy (if we exempt those who are "hired out" to big
business). In a study that appeared more than a decade
ago, two American social scientists argued that the most
"integrationist" elite was the leadership of big
business, which appeared to have made the greatest
strides in "laying to rest the two major ideological
codes -- nationalism and socialism -- which had shaped

political thinking... for centuries past."[15] This elite, moreover, which recognized that Western Europe had become not only "a permanent component of the Euramerican system," but more specifically of "Euratlantic Unlimited,"[16] has tended to speak English as well as the universal language of a commitment to growth and prosperity. We must, however, be careful about putting too much faith in this elite for promoting Euro-Atlanticism. The most prominent leaders of business are leaders of multinational corporations, and hence, while not particularly committed to the USA, or to France or Germany, they are not committed to Atlanticism either; they are essentially apatride in their attitudes: they are interested in profits, in international trade, and in the rationality of efficiency and productivity; they are anti-Communist, but they may have convergent cautionary notions[17] regarding the problems of (an excess of) democracy. This elite, which cannot be properly controlled either by the USA or any European country, is not Atlanticist but "Trilateralist." (It may be suggested here by some that Japan belongs to the "Euratlantic region;" and that the Japanese are honorary Euro-Americans becasue their elite is heavily composed of dynamic businessmen who speak English and appreciate good European cuisine; but the fact remains that they came to appreciate Euro-Atlantic socio-political values relatively late, that the essence of their civilization is oriental, and that they are a bigger commercial threat to Western Europe and the USA than these two regions are to one another.)

The American and Western European elites do not necessarily use the capacity to take the broader view which their education, their contacts, and their mobility have given them. More frequently, they disseminate stereotypes that cannot be conducive to the promotion of a Euro-Atlantic consciousness. Some years ago, an American[18] suggested that the Europeans viewed Americans as youthful and vigorous but callow and naive, and their culture as derivative; and that the Americans viewed Europeans as experienced and wise but also tired and decadent, but thought their culture original. He added that Americans are viewed by both as future-oriented, and Europeans by both as oriented toward the past. Such stereotypes are a source of comfort to their purveyors but they distort reality. Thus the American political system is older than that of any Western European polity (at least on the continent); while most Western European nations have given themselves new constitutions only recently, and have experimented with new political institutions, new decision-making patterns, and new political parties, Americans have contented themselves (or have been saddled) with an antique constitution and with ideologies more appropriate to the 19th than to the 20th century. As for culture, both American and European civilization contain original and derivative elements; but while the American elite is neither self-conscious nor apologetic about the fact that American culture is, in many essentials, a transplanted European one, significant elements of the European elite -- and in particular intellectuals -- appear to be uncomfortable, if not hysterical, about the allegedly pernicious consequences of American influences. To some Europeans (notably the French), what is most to be deplored -- and what has helped to embitter Franco-American relations -- is the "polluting"[19] impact of the Americans on the French language. A well-known European commentator (and devout Atlanticist) has recently lamented the confluence of several things allegedly American, or American-inspired -- all of which create a feeling of angst (sic) in Europeans, and especially in young Germans: soulless technology, vulgarity and superficiality, environmental pollution,[20] the danger of nuclear weapons, and "inauthentic food." (Whether it is really angst, or rather indigestion, that American food produces in Germans, it seems clear that, in the interest of fostering a truly Euro-Atlantic community, American efforts at diffusion must not involve American cuisine!) What still others criticize about Americans is their dissemination of mass culture, their emphasis on gadgetry, and their promotion of Philistine plutocrats to positions of leadership -- largely, one suspects, because all these developments, when they come to Europe, threaten the customary class distinctions and imperil the social positions of the traditional elite of aristocrats, humanists, and legalists.

There is another kind of critique, which expresses the Europeans' feeling that Americans are no longer true to themselves and which therefore reflects disappoint-ment over unfulfilled expectations. Americans are supposed to be pragmatic, but President Reagan's foreign policies -- or the rhetorical flourishes that often substitute[21] for them -- are wrapped in moralism and dogmatism. Americans are supposed to be innovative and adaptable, but they have failed to bring their institutions and policies up to date. Michel Crozier, for example, argues -- not without a touch of condescension -- that in the USA there is an excessive emphasis on individualism and private material satisfactions, that educational, cultural, and moral standards have declined, that "the melting pot no longer works," and that there are too many pressure groups whose existence aggravates a system of decision making that is already subject to too many blockages.[22]

The USA also seems to have failed to live up to its reputation as an effective manager of a modern industrial economy. In 1967, when Jean-Jacques

Servan-Schreiber published Le défi américain, the USA
owned 27 percent of the world's financial reserves, and
Western Europe 58 percent
     By late 1974, the American share was down to 13
percent, while that of Western Europe had risen to 64
percent. Moreover, by the mid-1970s, the net per capita
income in the USA had been overtaken by the net per[23]
capita incomes in several Western European countries.
While in the 1960s Western Europeans were worried about
American economic imperialism, in the late 1970s they
were increasingly discussing -- with a bit of
schadenfreude, perhaps -- the decline of American
productivity and the loss of its markets not only to
themselves but also to Japan.
     Such arguments may be patronizing, and may be
accompanied by the Europeans' mythologies about their
own superiorities -- e.g., of their universities, their
cities, and their cuisine -- as well as by the illusion
that whatever the Americans have imported from France
recently -- such as "Englench," French confiture and
Beaujolais sold in supermarkets, and bakeries "in
deepest California" baking baguettes -- has contributed[24]
to a "recul culturel de l'Amérique." At the same time,
it is painfully true that the USA has failed, to its own
detriment, to look seriously at Western European
institutional and policy innovations that represent a
considerable advance over existing American institutions
and policies, that might bring benefits to the American
public, and that might bring the USA and Western Europe
closer together.

The "Europeanization" of America: Possibilities and
Constraints
     An examination of European successes and American
failures would demonstrate that most of them have to do
with the relationship between public purposes and
private interests. The relative backwardness and
parsimony of the USA with respect to old-age pensions,
unemployment insurance, medical services, housing, and
many other types[25] of social benefits (with the exception
of education) could be explained in terms of the
anti-statist bias of Americans (sometimes reflected in
widespread gun ownership and the activities of vigilante
groups), the fear of "overloading" the government
machine, the existence of wide-open spaces and
opportunities, and the belief in the virtual
inexhaustibility of natural resources and hence the
possibility of unlimited growth. Having been spared
foreign invasions, hostile bombs, war-related social
dislocation, and mass starvation, and thus bereft of a
recent memory of national tragedy, America has not yet
been affected by Malthusian ideology. Now the fact that
the USA is no longer insulated from hostile (nuclear)
bombs and from dependence on foreign sources of energy

is likely to bring a "zero-sum" consciousness to academic economists and political decision-makers. Once this comes about, it is likely to be reflected in a greater sympathy for Western European approaches to the husbanding of resources and the "concerting" of the activities of the private sector.

For many years, the forces pushing for the welfare state have been weaker in the USA than in Western Europe: owing to the reality or myth of upward mobility, American labor unions were satisfied with the capitalist system and did nothing to foster working-class consciousness.[26] But the realization that the working class in Western Europe was at least as well off as in the USA; that American economic policy has been needlessly regressive (especially under the Reagan administration), and that the American worker has lost purchasing power more rapidly than his Western European counterpart -- all these might cause American labor leaders, who had hitherto been excessively concerned with anti-Communism, to look with greater appreciation at Western European models of economic decision making. Already some Americans[27] -- e.g., economists such as Walter Heller and politicians such as Hubert Humphrey, expressed some interest in European approaches to economic planning of the indicative (or "soft") variety; more recently, the appointment of the chief of the United Auto Workers to the board of directors of an automobile manufacturing firm opened vistas of a future for real industrial democracy in the USA. Certainly, the generalization of European-type worker-representation schemes in the USA would contribute greatly to Euro-American convergence, since it would improve the dialogue between American and European trade union spokesmen and would, at the same time, help to reduce the stumbling blocks to efforts of American industrialists to establish plants in Western Europe.

There are a number of recent policy innovations and interests in the USA that do show a European influence, but some of them, when adopted, have been, or are likely to be, so Americanized as to be -- insofar as Europeans are concerned -- distorted. Like Europeans, we have been rebuilding inner cities, but in doing so we have tended to replace residential with corporate structures. Like Western Europeans, we have toyed with the idea of formalized tripartite "elite management" of economic policy; but the Price-Wage Board set up in the early 1970s (by President Nixon) was a caricature of the Western European paritary ("social partnership") model, since business representatives outnumbered those of labor, and the wage freeze was not only imposed before bargaining began but was unaccompained by an effective price freeze. Periodically, American politicians and economists (generally of conservative inspiration) have considered the introduction of a value-added tax; such a tax would, however, be undesirable because its inherent regressivity is unlikely to be compensated (as in Western Europe) by meaningfully redistributive measures.

Some Western European policies are not likely to be adopted because of ideological or institutional constraints. The European system of monthly income supplements to families with children (allocation familiale or kindergeld) will not be instituted in the USA because the ideological underpinning for such a system -- the egalitarianism of socialism, the nationalism of Gaullism, or the familism of Catholic social doctrine -- is underdeveloped or absent. The adoption in the USA of a comprehensive system of medical coverage, which is now in effect in virtually all European countries, is impeded by several factors: the ideology of private doctor-patient relationships (which has been elevated from myth to deontology); the unified structure and immense wealth of organized medicine; and the fragmented nature of American decision making, which gives American physicians much greater veto power than has ever been possessed by their European counterparts. The building of mass rail transport systems in the USA has been impeded by three factors: the ideology of excessive individualism, which exalts private consumption over the production of social goods; the metropolitan sprawl, which has prevented the development of the critical population density to make rail systems profitable; and the political power of automobile manufacturers and oil companies.

The emulation of some Western European features by the USA, desirable though they may be, would be unthinkable. This is true of the classic parliamentary system, which provides continuity of leadership, furnishes a responsible opposition (a "shadow government"), introduces a note of constancy into domestic and foreign policies, and prevents novices from becoming chief policy-makers. There have always been Americans who have favored such a system: they have concluded that the hallowed American Constitution, with its checks and balances, may make for policy blockages, encourage pork-barrel politics, and produce inferior leadership.

It is clearly unrealistic to expect a significant "Europeanization" of the USA in the foreseeable future. The reason for this is not merely the kind of ethno-centrism that one associates with most nation-states. Rather, the explanation for the reluctance of Americans to learn from Europeans must be found in the notion of self-sufficiency and the idea of American exceptionalism: the conviction that European solutions to problems, European patterns and institutions, are old-fashioned and backward, or not quite democratic, and somehow cannot apply to a more "advanced" and more fortunate country (God used to live

in France, but in the 20th century he apparently became
a naturalized American). It is seen in the attitude of
American public-policy specialists: when they parade
concrete policy options, these are not likely to be
taken from Europe but from "internal" sources -- from
the experiences of American states, counties, and
cities, It is seen in the behavior of congressmen: they
go on junkets to Europe ostensibly for purposes of
"fact-finding," but what they bring back to the USA are
perfumes and cognacs, and not public-policy ideas to be
put into the legislative hopper. Similarly, when
American academics see certain "un-American" patterns of
representation, bargaining, and institutionalization
involving interest groups which are widespread in
Europe, they tend to assign misleading anti-democratic
labels to them (e.g., "corporatism", as distinct from
genuine pluralism) -- as if to suggest the essential
unfitness of these patterns for American use.[28]

Eventually, American policy-makers will look more
seriously to Western Europe -- not because of a sudden
fondness for European models but in response to internal
or external pressures, The skyrocketing costs of a
medical care delivery system based on entrepreneurialism
-- aggravated by the growth of the proportion of the
aged -- will make the introduction of some form of
statuatory medical coverage inescapable; another round
of large-scale oil price extortion by a revitalized OPEC
cartel may make a coherent network of mass rail
transport inevitable; a growing number of redundant
workers whose retraining the private sector has refused
to finance may force the government to embrace a more
active labor-market policy; and the increasing
inefficiency of monopolistic or oligopolistic private
sectors which have shown an unlimited capacity to absorb
"welfare payments" (e.g., the passenger railroad
service) will be so apparent that the government will
assume greater control over them. To be sure, the
ideological constraints to an American emulation of
European patterns will be such that the USA is highly
unlikely to opt for fully "socialized" medicine or for
the outright nationalization of decrepit companies.

The development of a non-military Atlanticism is
impeded by non-ideological factors as well. There have
been exaggerated expectations of a spillover from the
military component of NATO itself; a proof that NATO has
been an inadequate role model for harmonization
processes is that under it even such a prosaic matter as
weapons standardization has not been achieved. Moreover,
there is little sense in current American attempts to
salvage the military element of Atlanticism by putting
renewed stress on conventional warfare. In the first
place, such a stress only underlines America's
reluctance to use its strategic weapons in defense of
Europe and envisages the confinement of a future

Soviet-American conflict to the European battlefield;
second, the kind of updating of troop training and
weaponry that a usable conventional war machine implies
would require a much greater financial outlay than most
Western European countries are able or willing to
afford; and third, given its own fiscal deficit, the USA
is unlikely to underwrite this modernization.

Another problem is the fact that there has been a
lack of symmetry and clarity regarding America's
expectations of Europe, and vice-versa. An American
diplomat[29] has argued that Americans want a unified
Europe that is strong enough to resist the Russians but
not so strong as to harm American interests. This is the
obverse of Western Europeans' ambivalence: they want a
USA strong enough to help protect them from the
Russians, which means a USA stronger than any
combination of Western European countries -- but a USA
that does not stress its hegemonial position -- whose
strength is obvious to the USSR but not obtrusive to
Western Europeans.

Still another problem has been the simultaneous
existence of differential definitions of Atlanticism
embraced by Americans and Europeans, with each camp
bringing its own inclusionary and exclusionary approach
to the concept. The American notion of non-military --
i.e., commercial -- Atlanticism has sometimes been
annoying to Western Europeans in that it has included
Japan and thus threatened to "thin out" and denature its
meaning. The American tendency to extend Atlanticism
beyond the Atlantic area is particularly objectionable
to the Western European Left: for them the confusion of
the Atlantic defense community specifically, and
"Atlantic civilization" generally, with the management
of economic relations among the rich industrial
democracies is a reflection of the multinationals' view
of the globe, as articulated by the Trilateral
Commission. A leader of the German Social Democratic
Party has recently reminded the USA that NATO is neither
a global union, nor does Japan belong to NATO, nor would
West Germany wish to be tied, by virtue of its NATO
membership, "into a world-wide strategy of
confrontation."[30] On the other hand, Western Europeans
have had their own -- in effect "counter-trilateralist"
-- model, which reflects the belief that Western Europe
should play the role of intermediary between the USA and[31]
other regions, especially the Middle East and Africa.
(A specific example of this is the Giscardian idea of le
trialogue -- a triadic system of interactions among the
OPEC bloc as energy suppliers, the industrial
democracies as manufacturers and armorers, and finally
the Third World, with France playing a central
coordinating role.) At best, this kind of Western
European role playing has served as a vehicle for the
assertion of the national diplomatic importance of

France, West Germany, Britain, etc., or the "ego trips" of their leaders; at worst, it has had a destabilizing and destructive effect -- as did, for example, the Venice Declaration of 1980, which helped to undermine the Camp David agreement between Egypt and Israel. Euro-Atlanticism has also been subverted by the behavior, if not the very existence, of the European Economic Community which, instead of serving as a bridge between individual European countries and the USA, is perceived by the latter as a protectionist bloc that tries to impede American economic access to Western Europe. To some extent, the anti-American bias of the EEC is counterbalanced by the desire of each of the major Western European nations -- all the while endorsing the idea of European unity -- to have a privileged relationship with the USA, but for different reasons: the British, because of linguistic commonality; the French, because of historic ties of friendship, based on political affinities; the West Germans, because of their position as the "advance guard" of NATO (referred to above); and the Italians, because of strong ethnic bonds with a large number of Americans. Such bilateralist ideas have been given substance by the fact that, for the past 35 years, the relationship between the USA and individual European nations in many fields -- natural and social science, art, literature, student and faculty exchanges, etc. -- has been closer than that which has existed among these nations. Still, Euro-Atlanticism would have taken hold much more easily if it were not constantly muddied by the existence of other axial systems or pseudo-systems; or by the attempts of particular nations at "stretching" Western Europe to suit their own narrow concerns: e.g., Japan by the USA, East Germany by West Germany, and (Francophone) Africa by France.

During the past two or three decades there has been a certain convergence by both the USA and Western Europe toward a similar state of affairs that is neither inherently European nor American but is, rather the consequence of socio-economic "development" and is implicit in the nature of Western democratic mass politics. Both regions are concerned with what Irving Kristol has termed "prosaic domesticity" [33]: they tend to construe national interest in terms of material welfare or other concrete payoffs, i.e., in terms of dealing successfully with fiscal deficits, unemployment, employment, inflation, pollution, and the decline in productivity. Both regions now have the military in shackles (that is, under civilian control), and therefore "diplomacy by other means" -- the option traditionally chosen by large states -- no longer suggests itself easily. Finally, as both the USA and Western Europe have become more democratic and more responsive to the people, they have come to share what

Tocqueville has called the "structural deficiency" of democracies: the inability to pursue long-term domestic and foreign policies. For all these reasons, both the USA and Western European countries are easily subject to pressures of appeasement, and less capable psychologically to face the same triple challenge: the Soviet military threat, Japanese commercial pressures, and OPEC energy blackmail.

A Possible Agenda

Although the developments discussed above appear to serve as points d'appui for a non-military Atlanticism, they do not substitute for deliberate efforts at two-directional diffusion. Such efforts would have a number of components. Western Europeans might refrain from being "spoilers" of American policies, insofar as these policies do not affect the vital interests of European countries. Moreover, the Europeans' critique of American moralizing about Western European behavior might be more credible if Western Europeans moderated their own hypocrisies: one example is the Western European critique of Israeli "intransigence" and their simultaneous inability to notice the miscellaneous cruelties perpetrated in Arab countries; another is the Western European indignation about the violations of human rights in Latin American countries, indignation that is accompanied by a lack of energy in criticizing such violations in Communist countries (e.g., in connection with Soviet actions in Afghanistan, Jaruzelski's crackdown in Poland, and the discussions of "Basket Three" at the current conference on European security in Madrid).

For their part, Americans should be more sympathetic to Western European economic concerns. Some Western European demands, although their perfect reasonableness may be doubted, should nevertheless be taken more seriously for the sake of good will. Thus, France's recent call for a "new Bretton Woods conference" that would reinstitute stable exchange rates between the dollar and Western European currencies may be inconsistent with the French position in favor of free-floating exchange rates that had prevailed three or four years earlier, when the dollar was weak. But the French do have a point when they assert that intra-Atlantic financial solidarity is a two-way street. (In an address to the French Senate in the spring of 1983, Jacques Delors, the French Economic Affairs minister, reminded the Americans that "in 1978, when the sharp drop in /the value of the/ dollar unsettled the world economy, the industrialized nations got together $30 billion to support the American currency. But now the United States is not sending the elevator back up."[34]) Furthermore, it is in the American interest to alleviate the fiscal burden of the French (and Italian)

dependence on OPEC and to prevent a substitute
dependence on Soviet fuel supplies -- both of which have
a negative effect on Alliance solidarity. A genuinely
solidaristic behavior on the part of the USA would be a
formal commitment to share its fuel supplies with
Western Europe in the event of another Middle Eastern
oil embargo. It might also include a willingness to
permit West Europeans to supply a far larger proportion
than the present 20$_{35}$percent of the conventional
equipment of NATO forces -- a willingness that would
make the new American emphasis on NATO conventional
forces more appealing and perhaps also render the
reckless sale of military hardware to dictatorial or
unstable Third-World countries less financially
compelling for Western Europeans.

It is clear that Euro-Atlantic convergence would
require a settlement of disagreements over economic
issues. Both the USA and Western Europe are
protectionist; it is a matter of controversy which is
more so.$_{36}$ Discrimination against the USA which,
according to a European scholar, "was inherent in the
formation of a customs union among the countries of the
European Economic Community,"$_{37}$ was accepted by the USA
in the hope that the EEC would become a political union
which would introduce greater stability in Europe and
strengthen the West in general in relations with the
USSR. The EEC, however, fulfilled neither the political
hopes of the USA nor the economic expectations of the
Europeans. Even after the creation of an enlarged market
with the Third World (the Yaounde and Lome conventions)
and EFTA, and the establishment of the Common
Agricultural Policy -- arrangements that are perceived
to be discriminatory against the USA -- the USA
continued to maintain a trade surplus with the EEC.

Since NATO has failed to produce the hoped-for
Euro-Atlantic unity, and since the EEC has not given the
Western Europeans sufficient economic clout to keep the
USA out of Europe, it might be desirable for both the
Europeans and the Americans to enlarge the EEC with the
inclusion of the USA, i.e. to "Atlanticize" this
economic community. In this "Atlantic Economic
Community" the American presence, in terms of manpower,
capital and technology would doubtless be significant,
but not necessarily overwhelming. The old Gaullist fear
that American investment in Western Europe would lead to
American economic domination of the region has already
proved to be exaggerated; in recent years, much of
America's excess capital has gone to cheap-labor areas
in Third-World countries -- a development that has
caused American labor to mount a (somewhat futile)
effort at preventing the outflow of capital. Moreover,
there has been a compensatory European investment in the
USA -- e.g., the establishment of Volkswagen plants in
the USA and the buying up of shares in American

automobile plants by Renault -- a development that may
be attributed both to rising interest rates in the USA
and rising labor costs in Europe. Western European
governments should now redouble their efforts -- by
means of one or another kind of formalized relationship
between the EEC and the USA -- to encourage American
investments in Western Europe, for that would create a
degree of American financial involvement that would tie
the USA indissolubly to the fate of a capitalist Western
Europe. To many US decision-makers, the loss of billions
of American investment dollars that would follow a
Soviet takeover of the region would be more unbearable
-- and cry out louder for revenge -- than the battle
deaths of several thousand American "hostages"
(especially if a large proportion of them turned out to
be Blacks or Chicanos).

The USA might hesitate to join this enlarged
economic community, despite the new markets that would
be opened up to American products. For some Americans,
this hesitation would have an economic basis: the fear
that in certain areas -- mass transport, energy-saving
technology, and some electronic and chemical sectors --
European products would pose too much of a challenge.
For others, there is the fear that the USA would have to
subject itself to a supranational authority and lose
much of its sovereignty. But sovereignty is relative:
the American government's freedom of action has been
undermined by its dependence on the good will of Saudi
Arabia, the rationality of Soviet decision-makers, the
patriotism of leaders of multi-national corporations,
and the public-spiritedness of a myriad of internal veto
groups. On the other hand, many Americans would welcome
such membership, since it would force the public
authorities in the USA to adhere to Common-Market social
policy norms that are generally more progressive than
American ones.

Since the likelihood of the USA joining such an
enlarged community is slim, one must hope that a
non-military Atlantic community might evolve in the
manner of the Nordic Council: in this Scandinavian
regional grouping, the institutional framework is
sparse, and formal supra-nationality hardly exists; yet
owing to ideological homogeneity, frequent consultations
at various levels, and a complex network of transactions
among the member nations, legal standardization,
socio-economic harmonization, and cultural integration
have been achieved to a considerable extent. This kind
of evolution would be facilitated if the Western
Europeans and Americans adopted part of the other's
ideology: if the former became more American by
dismantling part of the tradition of etatism and moving
in the direction of libertarian pluralism (as
Dahrendorf, Jean-Francois Revel and assorted Giscardists
have suggested), and the latter became more European (or

more German, by embracing a proto-Hegelian idealism, as
David Calleo has argued[38]). Whether this kind of
"Americanization" or "Germanization" is desirable is a
moot question. In any case, a thorough ideological
convergence would be the consequence of, rather than the
precondition for, a Euro-Atlantic diffusion effort,
which would require the following concrete steps:

1. Massive American investment in Western Europe,
and Western European investment in the USA;

2. Arrangements that would facilitate EEC-USA trade,
such as the moderation of protective clauses by the EEC
that are blatently anti-American (e.g. agricultural
export subsidies) and the abolition by the USA of the
"American Selling Price" and other policies that are
construed as anti-European;

3. Frequent, perhaps semi-annual, Euro-Atlantic
(rather than Trilateral) summit conferences involving
American and Western European chief executives, and
parallel conferences of ministers of economics,
education, labor, social affairs, etc., which would aim
at the coordination of foreign, industrial, trade, and
social policies, and would enable one side to learn from
the successes and failures of the other;

4. Regular and more or less formalized meetings of
trade-union officials, city planners, social
administrators, scientists, and other specialists;

5. The exchange of scholars -- in both directions --
who know the language of the host country well, and who
do not necessarily have the imprimatur of either the
State Department or the Atlantic Institute.

The diffusion of ideas and policies is not to be
understood as merely a matter of deliberate government
policy. A major responsiblity should lie with non-
governmental organizations, private foundations, educational establishments and business -- all of which could
contribute to the dissemination of common values[39] and
the cultivation of a "Euratlantic" consciousness.

In the 1950s and 1960s, there were Europeans who
believed that the mere existence of NATO would insure a
deep American political commitment to Western European
integrity: since all NATO commanders-in-chief have been
American, these have tended to argue the importance of a
Western European orientation on the highest levels,
particularly after they returned to the USA and assumed
political office. Today, there may be Americans who are
convinced that there is little need for deliberate
efforts at non-military diffusion, since military
Atlanticism has gotten a reprieve in Britain, France and
West Germany with the election, respectively, of
Thatcher, Mitterrand, and Kohl. But since not all NATO
chiefs become President (like Eisenhower) or Secretary
of State (like Haig), and since the three major Western
European nations may eventually elect leaders who will

32

be hostile to military Atlanticism, a more deliberate
effort at creating a non-military Euro-Atlantic system
may be indispensable. In such a system, pattern
similarities will be so obvious, and transactions so
intertwined, that both Western Europeans and Americans
will feel themselves to be part of a common
civilization, and that the Euro-American relationship
will no longer be capable of disentanglement without
unacceptable loss. In short, it will be in the
self-interest of the USA -- and will be perceived as
such by the Western European nations and by the USSR --
to defend Western Europe in the same way that it would
defend one of the American states. This would be the
ultimate guarantee of Western European security.

NOTES

1. Ronald Steel, "The Abdication of Europe," in
Atlantis Lost, ed. by James Chace and Earl C. Ravenal
(New York: New York University Press, 1976), pp. 47-63.
2. William Pfaff, "Sinking into Materialism," New
Yorker, March 30, 1981.
3. A.W. De Porte, Europe Between the Superpowers
(New Haven and London: Yale University Press, 1979), p.
213. See also Pierre Lellouche, "Does NATO Have a
Future?", The Washington Quarterly, Summer, 1982, pp.
40-52, who argues that NATO as presently constituted
must either be changed, or it will die.
4. Henry Kissinger, "Something is Deeply Wrong in
the Atlantic Alliance," Washington Post, December 21,
1981.
5. A. Haig, "NATO and Restoring US Leadership,"
Current Policy Paper No. 276, State Department,
Washington, D.C., May 9, 1981.
6. Cf. Dean Acheson's critique of Gaullist policies
as reflecting "atavistic mysticism in Europe: Decision
or Drift?", Atlantic Community Quarterly, Spring, 1966,
p. 20.
7. Thus the argument in Stanley Hoffmann (Gulliver's
Troubles, New York: McGraw-Hill, 1968), who tends to
reflect a "Gaullist" viewpoint, and for whom the USA
either overuses its power, or does not use it
effectively or intelligently enough -- i.e., in
accordance with French (Gaullist) preferences.
8. See the perceptive article by David Andelman,
"Struggle over Western Europe," Foreign Policy, Winter
1982-1983, pp. 37-51.

9. There was also a (perhaps unconscious) admiration on the part of certain members of the American elite of German efficiency in solving problems -- e.g., problems of modernization, the integration of refugees, unemployment, and the problem of minorities...though not all of this may be openly acknowledged.

10. According to Douglas Eden, the West Germans have helped to maintain the Atlantic community, while the French have tried to destroy it. "Enjoying the luxury of American protection at virtually no cost, and buffered against the Soviet world by West Germany, French diplomats belittle the United States and flirt with the Soviet Union in the cause of French 'independence'." Eden, "The Alliance Under Stress: National Interests and Political Change," in Eden and Short, eds., Political Change in Europe (New York: St. Martin's, 1981), p. 155. Eden ignores the fact that a) for many years it was Germany that got protection without furnishing its own meaningful military or financial contribution; b) it was Germany, not France, that flirted with the USSR by initiating Ostpolitik; and c) that France has been edging closer to NATO while West Germany has shown increasing signs of neutralism.

11. Brzezinski, "The European Crossroads," in Atlantis Lost, pp. 85-102.

12. For example, the Declaration of the Rights of Man in 1789, which was probably influenced by the Virginia Bill of Rights of 1776.

13. On the growing role of the mass media in French politics, see Monica Charlot, "The Language of Television Campaigning," in France at the Polls, ed. by Howard R. Penniman (Washington, D.C.: American Enterprise Institute, 1975), pp. 227-253.

14. Cf. the interview with Theodore Lowi by Annick Percheron, "La Science politique americaine decouvre l'etat," Le Monde de Dimanche, January 3, 1982.

15. Daniel Lerner and Morton Gorden, Euratlantica: Changing Perspectives of the European Elites, (Cambridge, Mass.: MIT Press, 1969), p. 288.

16. Ibid., p. 296f.

17. See Michel Crozier, Samuel Huntington, and Joji Watanuki, The Crisis of Democracy: Report on the Governability of Democracies to the Trilateral Commission (New York: New York University Press, 1975).

18. Eric Larrabee, "Transcripts of a Transatlantic Dialogue," in A New Europe? ed. by S. Graubard (Boston: Beacon Press, 1967), pp. 526-537.

19. Cf. René Etiemble, Parlez-vous franglais? (Paris: Gallimard, 1964). 20. Pierre Hassner, "The Shifting Foundation," Foreign Policy No. 48 (Fall, 1982), especially 6-8.

21. Andelman, loc. cit., pp. 47f.

22. Michel Crozier, Le mal américain (Paris: Fayard, 1980), pp. 286-88.

23. Figures cited in Robert Heller and Norris Willat, The European Revenge (New York: Scribners, 1975), p. 7.

24. Crozier, Le mal américain pp. 293-4.

25. See Anthony King, "Ideas, Institutions, and Policies of Governments: A Comparative Analysis," British Journal of Political Science 3 (July and October 1973), 291-313, 409-423.

26. Cf. Andrew Martin, The Politics of Economic Policy in the United States (Beverly Hills: Sage Publications, 1973).

27. Cf. Walter Heller, New Dimensions of Political Economy (New York: Norton, 1967), pp. 51-57.

28. For a discussion, see William Safran, "Interest Groups in Three Industrial Democracies: France, West Germany, and the United States," in Constitutional Democracy: Essays in Comparative Politics. Festschrift in honor of Henry W. Ehrmann, ed. by Fred Eidlin (Boulder, Co.: Westview Press, 1983).

29. J.R. Schaetzel, "Das Europabild der Amerikaner," in Amerika und Westeuropa, ed. Karl Kaiser and Hans-Peter Schwarz (Stuttgart and Zurich: Belser Verlag, 1977), pp. 29-40.

30. Johannes Rau, vice-chairman of the SPD, cited in Deutschland-Nachrichten Nr. 21, 01.06.1983.

31. Cf. Pierre Hassner, "Die amerikanische Weltmacht und die Westeuropäischen Mächte," in Kaiser and Schwarz, op. cit., p. 313.

32. See Francois Bondy, "Kultur als Brücke," in Kaiser and Schwarz, op. cit., p. 79.

33. Irving Kristol, "Does NATO Exist?" in NATO: The Next Thirty Years, ed. by Kenneth A. Myers (Boulder, Co.: Westview Press, 1980), p. 368.

34. News and Comments From France, French Embassy, Press and Information Service, April 21, 1983.

35. See "Bonn Balks at Weinberger's Arms Plans," New York Times, June 1, 1983.

36. See Martin Baron, "Protectionism: Nobody's Perfect," Europe, March-April 1983, pp. 10-12.

37. Karl Kaiser, Europe and the United States: The Future of the Relationship (Washington, D.C.: Columbia Books, 1973), p. 17.

38. David Calleo, "Should We Be More German?", Spectator, January 13, 1979.

39. Cf. the steps advocated by the Atlantic Council in The Teaching of Values and the Successor Generation, Atlantic Council of the United States, Policy Papaers, Washington D.C., February 1983.

3. Arms Control and Security: The Federal Republic and the European Order

Wolfram F. Hanrieder

There is a striking continuity in the Federal Republic's concerns with matters that are roughly, but inadequately, circumscribed by the term "security." Most issues of the 1980s are rooted in past decades, which attest to the durability of the military and political division of Europe and the Federal Republic's security dependence on the United States, as well as to the abiding connections between national security policy and diplomacy, between arms and politics.

Throughout the thirty-five year history of the North Atlantic Treaty Organization the central military doctrine of NATO was that of strategic deterrence, which served as the military-strategic implementation of the overarching American political strategy of containment. Containment and deterrence were mutually reinforcing elements of an American strategy that faced, at the divide of Europe, toward both East and West: it was intended to check the Soviet Union at the same time as it established in Western Europe the geopolitical basis on which the American Cold War effort could be securely emplaced.

Just as containment embodied a dual component -- one directed toward the Soviet Union, the other toward the Federal Republic -- so did deterrence. While one component of American deterrence policy was aimed at the Soviet Union, threatening dire consequences in case of Soviet aggression, an equally important component was aimed at America's West European allies: that of reassuring them that their security interests were adequately accommodated by the first component. Together, the threat of punishing the opponent and the attending reassurance effect on the allies, made up the core of the transatlantic security partnership and underlined America's determination to contain the Soviet Union.

In the immediate postwar years, the deterrence and containment aspects of American strategy were complimentary and mutually reinforcing, not only in their dimensions that were directed toward the Soviet

Union but also in those directed toward the Federal
Republic. Containment of the Soviet Union and
containment of the Federal Republic was accomplished
through the same mechanisms, primarily the creation of
integrative transatlantic and West European military and
political-economic institutions that bound the Federal
Republic to the West at the same time as they laid the
foundations for a concerted Western posture vis-à-vis
the Soviet Union. In the military-strategic realm,
deterring the Soviet Union and reassuring the Western
allies was equally compatable, largely because the
American commitment to extend deterrence to Western
Europe and protect its security rested on the secure
foundation of American nuclear superiority.

In later years, the dual components of both
containment and of deterrence began to diverge. With
respect to the American policy of double-containment,
some Germans began to question the static view of the
European order this policy implied, above all for the
division of Germany; and the deterring and reassuring
aspects of America's policy of deterrence also became
less complimentary as the gradual diminution of the West
Europeans' confidence that the United States would risk
national suicide for the sake of the alliance. As the
Soviet Union began to reach nuclear parity with the
United States and as the idea of extended deterrence
became less convincing, the dual principles of
deterrence and of reassurance -- on whose complemen-
tarity the common purpose and cohesion of the Atlantic
security community ultimately rested -- began to
diverge. As a consequence, NATO began to suffer from a
central dilemma which could not be resolved: the United
States, in seeking to limit the arms race and arrive at
a stable nuclear balance, was compelled to deal with the
Soviet Union on the basis of parity, as was reflected in
the arrangements of the Strategic Arms Limitation Talks
(SALT) and the ongoing Strategic Arms Reduction Talks
(START). At the same time, Washington could not
convincingly guarantee the security of Western Europe
except on the basis of an implied American nuclear
superiority.

Neither the United States nor the European NATO
allies can be blamed for this dilemma; and it is
unlikely that such a dilemma could have been escaped.
Developments in weapons technology and Soviet
determination to catch up with the United States brought
about nuclear parity between the two superpowers. Parity
and its implications led to conflict between the United
States (which now needed to take into account the
potential nuclear devastation of the United States and
therefore sought to delay the use of nuclear weapons)
and NATO partners at the forward line of defense, such
as the Federal Republic, who found unacceptable a

strategy that implied sustained conventional warfare at the expense of their territory and population.

Given the relative decline of American power, it would appear that the security of the United States and Western Europe is much more precarious in the early 1980s than it was in the late 1940s. But the meaning of security also changed during the intervening decades. Most fundamentally, traditional security concerns -- understood as the preservation of territorial integrity against outside intrusion -- have diminished relative to economic issues. Although security can turn into a question of national survival in the nuclear age -- and in that sense is unsurpassed in importance -- a noticeable shift of emphasis has taken place in world politics, away from the primacy of military-strategic elements of power toward the primacy of economic elements. The likelihood of invasions and direct military aggression across alliance boundaries has receded (the military prowess of the Soviet Union is felt more keenly by her partners than her adversaries), and this is especially true in areas of the world where existing borders are uncontested and unambiguous. For a variety of reasons, highly industrialized countries are not attractive targets for physical aggression and territorial occupation; and, except in parts of the nonindustrialized world and the Middle East, demands for territorial revisions are not pressing issues in contemporary international politics, the Falkland War of 1982 notwithstanding.

As the immediacy and intensity of the Soviet threat diminished in the eyes of both Europeans and Americans, their governments shifted priorities from strategic-military matters to political and economic ones, and centrifugal pressures were allowed a freer rein within the Western alliance. American planners still saw NATOs primary function as military, but by the middle 1960s they no longer considered a Warsaw Pact assault on Western Europe probable and were devoting most of their attention to Vietnam. Gradually Washington supplemented its Cold War policy of region-by-region, "forward" containment with attempts to reach a bilateral accommodation with the Soviet Union on matters of overriding mutual interest, such as stabilization of the global strategic balance of power. Containment at the periphery of the alliance blocs was augmented by a core of détente, as exemplified in the Strategic Arms Limitation Talks.

West Europeans, with a similarly relaxed view of the Soviet military threat, began to see the primary function of NATO as political -- that is, ensuring a continued US commitment to the political and economic future of Europe and thus ultimately guaranteeing the continent's military security also. As the West Europeans undertook their own political and economic arrangements with the East bloc, intra-European détente and its dynamics for overcoming the East-West division sometimes conflicted with the more static strategic détente between the two superpowers (which merely stabilized the East-West division). The United States had to deal with the Soviet Union on the basis of recognizing the status quo in Europe, but many Europeans on both sides of the dividing line were seeking to overcome it.

These strategic, political and psychological developments had a profound impact on the meaning of national security and on the purposes and instruments of arms control. As the likelihood of war in Europe diminished, the Western powers could afford to use military terms to express what were at bottom political concerns. Security policies, strategic doctrines, and arms control proposals became saturated with purposes that were essentially political rather than military. The logic of power was being expressed in the language of security and arms control. By the mid-sixties most of the major participants in the East-West dialogue on arms control had begun to use security policy to articulate and advance political objectives.

The Peculiarities of the German Situation

The political uses of strategic language and arms control proposals, and the general shift from military elements of power toward economic ones, were especially important to West Germany, for several reasons. First, because of its geography and history, from the beginning the Federal Republic was a NATO member with special inhibitions, obligations, anxieties, and opportunities. Whatever problems plagued NATO because of waning American nuclear superiority always were felt more keenly in Bonn than in other West European capitals. Because of legal, political and psychological restrictions, the Federal Republic could not supplement its security connection with the United States by establishing a nuclear deterrent of its own -- as had France and the United Kingdom -- and they had relatively little influence in the nuclear management of the alliance on which their ultimate security depended. These considerations alone would have made it difficulat for the Germans to express political purposes in military-strategic language. But there were other inhibitions as well. Because of Germany's past, had the West Germans followed General de Gaulle's example of couching political aspirations in terms of arms, they would have been accused of being unreconstructed militarists. Especially sensitive to the question of any kind of German association with nuclear weapons -- the German finger on the nuclear trigger. Whenever German policy touched upon nuclear matters -- talks about a Franco-German nuclear consortium in the early

1960s, Germany's participation in the proposed
multilateral nuclear NATO force, Bonn's footdragging on
the nonproliferation treaty -- anxiety levels rose in
the West as well as in the East. The Germans had to
speak softly indeed. This applied also to the recurring
suggestions, which were endorsed as well as opposed
within the Federal Republic, to enlarge the geographical
area of NATO's security concerns for purposes of
safeguarding energy supplies (especially in the Middle
East and Persian Gulf region) so as to match a broader
definition of security with a broader commitment for its
defense.

The case of West Germany is a special one for a
second reason: the Federal Republic was one of the main
political beneficiaries of the shift from military
elements of power to economic-monetary elements. Aside
from the fact that Germany's political and diplomatic
leverage increased as its economic and monetary strength
grew, economic and monetary "language" provided the
Germans with an excellent opportunity to translate
political demands -- which might still have been suspect
because of Germany's past -- into respectable economic
demands. Although the Germans grumbled a good deal about
the fact that they were always called upon to pay
"subsidies" of one sort or another to one country or
another, the shift from military to economic elements of
power was highly advantageous to them. The
transformation of economic power into political power,
and the translation of political demands into economic
demands, compensated for the Germans' handicap of not
being able to translate political demands into
military-strategic language.

Above all perhaps, the Federal Republic found it
difficult to translate political purposes into the
language of strategic doctrine because of its guarded
view, in the 1950s and 1960s, of the ramifications of
East-West arms control.

The Federal Republic and Arms Control
As is the case with most German security issues, the
arms control concerns of the 1980s are linked with a
striking continuity to those of past decades. For those
who are old enough, déjà vu is a frequent occurence in
observing European, and especially German, attitudes on
arms control. The issues of the early 1980s -- the
political ramifications of the deployment of modernized
Soviet and American intermediate-range missiles in
Europe, the sensitivity to the political implications of
arms control, the concerns occasioned by revisions of
Washington's deterrence posture, the weary frustrations
engendered by the intractable and apparently
interminable negotiations over NATO and Warsaw Pact
conventional troop levels -- are all rooted in the
distant past of the 1950s. The basic reason for this is

fairly simple (perhaps because it is also somewhat
tautological), and is to be found in the remarkable
durability of the political and military division of
Europe, which was solidified in the mid-1950s with the
introduction of nuclear weapons to Europe and with the
integration of the two German states in their respective
military alliances. For Europeans, arms control
proposals have always held fundamental implications not
only for the stability of the European military balance
but also for the shape of the European political order.
    The history of West German attitudes toward arms
control is complex. Because of Germany's history, even
the shadow of a German finger on the nuclear trigger
casts a shadow; and the Germans' association with arms
remains vaguely threatening, even as they themselves
feel vaguely insecure. Although four decades have passed
since most of Europe suffered at the hands of German
military might, European sensitivities (both in the East
and in the West) have remained raw; and many Germans
themselves demonstrate a commendable moral sensibility
in their often uneasy relationship with military
matters, conventional or nuclear. But above all, the
torturous German response to the arms control proposals
of the fifties and sixties stemmed from political
misgivings over their repercussions on the issue of
Germany's division. The various proposals put forth in
the 1950s and 1960s by the East as well as by the West
played an important role in the East-West diplomacy on
the German question -- that is, on the political
configuration of the European order -- and they were
invariably freighted with implications for Bonn's
Eastern policies that the Germans found distasteful or
outright unacceptable. The need to assess the
implications of arms control proposals for the German
question distinguished the Federal Republic from other
European NATO members and strongly shaped German
attitudes on arms control proposals. The Federal
Republic's relations with its Eastern neighbors were
burdened by large unresolved issues, which stemmed from
the refusal of successive Bonn governments to recognize
the German Democratic Republic and to accept as
permanent, under international law, the Oder-Neisse
borderline between Poland and the German Democratic
Republic. Since most arms control proposals for Europe
implied the recognition of the European status quo, and
in some cases were specifically intended to serve that
purpose, the Germans responded to such proposals with
caution ranging on suspicion, with hesitation ranging on
procrastination and rejection.³
    The more accommodating attitude adopted by the Grand
Coalition government (1966-69), and especially its
successor, the Brandt government (1969-74), stemmed from
a realistic appraisal of the limits and opportunities of
German policy. The Brandt government, in particular, was

sensitive to the fact that German political interests would be ill-served by stalling European détente because it would bring with it a legitimization of the political status quo, that is, a legitimization of the East German state. Thus Bonn saw political advantages in backing détente and arms control measures, especially since the goals of German Ostpolitik necessitated adopting a more conciliatory attitude toward the East. The Brandt government's Ostpolitik also became a complementary part of the Federal Republic's security policies -- not because it lessened the Federal Republic's strategic dependence on the United States or its allegiance to NATO, but because Bonn's readiness to accept the territorial status quo tackled German security problems at their political roots. In contrast to the fifties and sixties, when Bonn's security policy conflicted sharply with its Eastern policy, Ostpolitik overcame these stark contradictions. By recognizing the territorial and political realities stemming from World War II, the Germans meshed their security policy and their Eastern policy, developed a more constructive attitude toward arms control, and adjusted West German foreign policy to the dynamics of East-West détente.

Détente and Western Security

Adjusting German diplomacy to the Western powers' détente policies of the early 1970s was not an easy matter, however. Even though Bonn's Ostpolitik followed rather than preceded other dynamic Western approaches to the East, their partners' initial response to Ostpolitik (especially in Washington) demonstrated to the Germans that their own approach called for a delicate balance of movement and restraint. Too little readiness to support East-West accommodation had in the past brought charges of obstructionism (especially when Bonn dragged its feet on arms control); too much enthusiasm for détente raised fears that Bonn would weaken its ties to the West to create better prospects for German unity. The suspicion that the Federal Republic was an actual or potential revisionist European power, prepared to unhinge the status quo if given the opportunity, was close to the surface of many of the issues -- political, military-strategic, economic -- that were contested between Bonn and other capitals. But for reasons of history, geography and the abiding issue of intra-German relations, the aspirations and hopes reflected in a Western policy of détente were especially pertinent to the Federal Republic; and the Brandt government was prepared to make the indispensable contribution to its success -- the acceptance of the European status quo -- and thus convey to the East, which had suffered at German hands perhaps more than the West, the same measure of political accommodation and moral sensibility that Adenauer had extended to the West. By attuning West

German foreign policy to the dynamics of détente -- the outstanding foreign policy aim of most members of the Warsaw Pact as well as of the Atlantic Alliance -- Bonn hoped to keep pace with developments and retain German leverage in an East-West setting in which various kinds of political, strategic, and economic issues were coupled in multilayered connections.

In the 1970s, especially after the issues of Afghanistan and Poland beclouded East-West relations, a major source of disagreement between the United States and Western Europe (and especially between the United States and the Federal Republic) was the fact that the meaning attached to détente was different on both sides of the Atlantic. In Europe, détente referred to one part of a dual strategy: that of conveying to the Soviet Union and Eastern Europe a readiness for dialogue, negotiations, and cooperation, while at the same time ensuring an adequate military balance between NATO and the Warsaw Pact. This so-called "two-pillar" concept recognized that a constructive and (in the long run) realistic Western policy of cooperation with the East would have to rest on the secure foundations of military preparedness so as to maintain the defensive capabilities of the Western Alliance.

But the results of détente were assessed quite differently in the United States and in Western Europe, in large part because the expectations that centered on détente were different. Those of the superpowers, had they been fully articulated, were contradictory to begin with -- the United States expected Soviet restraint in most areas of contention, while the Soviet Union sought primarily the solidification of the European status quo and increased economic relations with the Western powers. The Germans were perhaps the main beneficiaries of détente because their expectations of enlarged and intensified human contacts between the Federal Republic and the German Democratic Republic were at least partially fulfilled, and the Federal Republic managed as well to enhance its international prestige and diplomatic leverage. As a consequence, throughout the seventies the Germans remained committed to the evolution of a European order that would secure and broaden those benefits, while neither the United States nor the Soviet Union shared those benefits and embraced that commitment.

Security and Arms Control in the 1980s
In the late 1970s, the twenty-year-old issue of the East-West nuclear balance in Europe, dormant for a decade, became reconnected with the thirty-year old issues of forward defense, the timing of an American nuclear response, and the general reliability of the American nuclear commitment to Europe.

In the 1950s, when the United States deployed sixty intermediate-range Thor missiles in Britain and forty-five Jupiters in Italy and Turkey, it intended them (in contrast to the tactical nuclear weapons that were deployed in Central Europe at the same time) as an interim-measure until the development of American intercontinental missiles would permit the United States to cover the Soviet targets it thought necessary. By 1964, when the United States had obtained that capability, these missiles were withdrawn. The Soviet Union, which also had deployed a number of IRBMs in the 1950s, similarly viewed them as a compensatory device (mostly because technical problems slowed down the Soviet intercontinental missile program), but did not withdraw them once it had reached parity with the United States and began to modernize them in the 1970s with the deployment of the highly accurate, lower-yield, three-warhead SS-20s. Together with the development of a new intermediate-range nuclear bomber, the Backfire, the Soviet Union achieved a eurostrategic nuclear preponderance of awesome proportions, for which NATO's nuclear-armed aircraft and the French and British national nuclear contingents provided insufficient compensation.

It was, among Europeans, most prominently German Chancellor Helmut Schmidt who expressed concern over the growing eurostrategic nuclear imbalance in a much-noted speech in London in October 1977, in which he argued that nuclear parity, as institutionalized in the Strategic Arms Limitation Talks, had "neutralized" the nuclear capabilities of both sides and therefore magnified the significance of the disparities between East and West in tactical-nuclear and conventional weapons.(Even before Schmidt's speech, two NATO panels, one dealing with military aspects, the other with arms control aspects, had begun deliberations on the issues raised by the eurostrategic imbalance). But Schmidt's concerns stemmed primarily from political rather than strictly security considerations. The German government wished to retain a measure of influence in the ongoing SALT II negotiations and, in fact, had pressed Washington to include eurostrategic nuclear weapons in them. Having failed in that, the Schmidt government, expecting the ratification of SALT II in the American Senate, assumed that eurostrategic weapons would be dealt with in a subsequent round of arms control negotiations, already labeled SALT III. Initially, the Carter administration was not enthusiastic about the modernization of intermediate-range nuclear forces (INF), fearing further complications for the SALT II negotiations, but by the time of the Guadaloupe Big Four meeting of January 1979 there was already some preliminary agreement to modernize NATO's INF, which

became coupled, at the summit, with the idea to seek
arms control measures at the same time.

This culminated in December 1979 in NATO's so-called
"double-track" decision to deploy in Europe, beginning
in 1983, 572 American Pershing II missiles and cruise
missiles, capable of reaching the Soviet Union, and to
seek at the same time -- this was the second "track" --
arms control agreements with the Soviet Union that would
make the first part of the decision unnecessary. All of
the 108 Pershing missiles but only 96 of the cruise
missiles were to be deployed on German territory,
reflecting the determination of the German government --
based largely on political grounds -- that Germany would
not be the sole West European NATO member to host
weapons that the Soviet Union considered a major
strategic threat.[4]

The Security Dimension

For the Federal Republic's security interests, the
decision to deploy modernized intermediate-range nuclear
weapons carried contradictory implications. On the one
hand one could argue that an imbalance on an important
rung of the ladder of escalation (such as eurostrategic
systems) would, unless redressed, create a gap in the
flexible response posture of NATO and weaken the entire
Western deterrence strategy. Should NATO fail in
checking a Soviet attack with conventional forces and
resort to battle-field tactical nuclear weapons, the
accuracy and reduced yield of the Soviet SS-20s would
give Moscow the opportunity to escalate the conflict by
striking NATO's nuclear-equipped aircraft capable of
reaching the Soviet Union, presenting the United States
with the choice of doing nothing or resorting to
intercontinental nuclear weapons. On the other hand one
could argue that the restoration of the eurostrategic
nuclear balance would have the very opposite effect and
encourage the decoupling of the American strategic
deterrent from Europe: by substantially improving NATO's
capability to strike the Soviet Union from Western
Europe, the deployment of modernized theater nuclear
forces might give the United States the option to limit
a war to Europe.

Although not divorced from considerations of the
military strategic balance, either calculation rested,
at bottom, on political judgments about American and
Soviet intentions. For the Schmidt government -- and
especially for the Chancellor himself, who had become
increasingly skeptical about the circumspection and
consistency of American diplomacy in general and that of
the Carter administration in particular -- the
restoration of the eurostrategic military balance,
either through the deployment of modernized NATO weapons
or the reduction of Soviet weapons, was the essential
prerequisite for sustaining the European political

balance. The Germans wanted to see the bilateral Soviet-American strategic equilibrium which was in the process of being codified in the SALT II treaty, extended into the eurostrategic balance, which was being threatened by the rapid deployment of Soviet SS-20s. The extensive modernization plans for the 1980s of the British and French national nuclear arsenals, coupled with the extensive deployment of the Soviet SS-20s, threatened to make NATO the weakest nuclear presence in Europe, with the consequence that the Federal Republic (which had no alternative to the nuclear protection provided by NATO) would have suffered by comparison, politically as well as strategically. Tying down the American nuclear commitment to Western Europe was, to be sure, related to the question of whether a restored eurostrategic nuclear balance would promote either a strengthened coupling with the intercontinental central strategic weapons of the United States or, on the contrary, enhance American opportunities for limiting a nuclear war to Europe. But there was a "downward" connection to a lower rung of the ladder of escalation, which received little attention in the public debate and in the academic literature, but which may have been more important in German calculations than the "upward" escalatory linkage between NATO's eurostrategic systems and America's global strategic deterrent: maintaining (or restoring) the eurostrategic nuclear balance enhanced the credibility of the Federal Republic's conventional deterrent posture. Rough parity on the eurostrategic nuclear level would serve less as a <u>floor</u> from which to threaten an escalation upward (although it might serve that function, too) than a <u>ceiling</u> under which NATO's conventional forces would gain in importance since it diminished the incentive for either NATO or the Warsaw Pact to escalate the conflict to the nuclear level.

This was in the German interest for several reasons. Chancellor Schmidt had a high regard for the fighting capabilities of the German <u>Bundeswehr</u> (he considered them second only to that of the Israeli army), and he believed that this assessment was shared by the Soviet Union. Restoring the eurostrategic nuclear balance would, for the reasons indicated, increase the importance of conventional capabilities and thus maximize the German advantage, politically as well as for purposes of deterrence, provided by the efficiency of the German <u>Bundeswehr</u> The German "disadvantage" of not being a nuclear power could be compensated for by increasing the military and political importance of German conventional capabilities. Second, and perhaps even more important, in the late 1970s and early 1980s a number of influential Western analysts, fearing or anticipating the collapse of NATO under the weight of its unresolved issues, called for a sweeping

reorganization of NATO's organizational structure as
well as for a reshaping of its strategy that would face
squarely the implications for West European security of
U.S.-Soviet nuclear parity. Among other suggestions,
such as dropping NATO's longstanding option of
"first-use" of nuclear weapons, [5] some analysts argued
for a return to the "basics" of European security -- the
defense of national territory. This would serve not only
the political self-assertion of Western Europe and
lessen the grip of the superpowers on the European
political order but also relegate nuclear weapons to a
less obtrusive and more reassuring role. As Michael
Howard put it: "The necessity for /nuclear/
countermeasures should be fully and publicly explained,
but they should be put in the context of the fundamental
task which only non-nuclear forces can effectively carry
out -- the defense of territory. Nuclear deterrence
needs to be subordinated to this primary task of
territorial defense, and not vice versa."[6]
    The political implications of such a shift of
emphasis, especially if it were to be institutionalized
through a West European "diplomatic concert" on security
measures, would of course be enormous. It would require
the structural reform of NATO, enlarge the Europeans'
share of defense burdens, and obtain for Western Europe
-- and the Federal Republic -- a larger role in guiding
events toward a new European order.[7]

The Arms Control Dimension
    It was the political as well as the military-
strategic ramifications of the 1979 double-track
decision that became the focal point of German-American
security difficulties toward the end of the Schmidt
government and at the beginning of the Kohl government,
which took office in October 1982 and was reaffirmed by
a general election in March 1983.
    The Reagan administration found it extremely
difficult to persuade its European allies that it was
seriously committed to arms control. It placed known
opponents of the SALT II treaty in key positions in its
arms control agencies and negotiating teams; it raised
discussion about "protracted" nuclear war and America's
determination to "prevail" in it; and there was a
nagging suspicion in Europe, fueled by injudicious
American statements, that Washington aimed for nuclear
superiority over the Soviet Union and that the
deployment of missiles capable of reaching the Soviet
Union from Western Europe was one way of implementing
that intention.
    The latter point appeared to be especially
significant. The Reagan administration argued that the
United States was inferior to the Soviet Union on the
level of intercontinental strategic capabilities -- an
argument that the Schmidt government found implausible

and that the Kohl government chose to ignore in public
-- and that this new "window of vulnerability" should be
closed as quickly and tightly as possible. This was to
be accomplished, at great cost, with the continuing
improvement of the three components of the American
strategic triad. The sea-based leg was to be improved by
adding a new Trident nuclear-capable submarine each year
and, above all, by increasing the accuracy of sea-based
missiles by the late 1980s. The air-based leg was to be
improved by the development of the B-1 bomber, as an
interim solution until a multi-purpose bomber with a
strategic range and "stealth" technology could be
deployed by the late 1980s or early 1990s, and by
modifying the existing B-52 bomber fleet to accommodate
air-launched cruise missiles. The major problem was the
intended modernization of the land-based leg of the
triad. The technological and political infirmities of
the MX program (both connected with the insoluble
problem of choosing a plausible basing mode) made it an
unsatisfactory method for modernizing the Minuteman
missile complex; and the proposed supplementary
development of a large number of single-warhead
Midgetman missiles with a mobile basing mode suggested a
revamping of the American negotiation position in the
START negotiations. In any case, the modernization plans
for any of the three legs of the triad could not be
implemented until the late 1980s at the earliest.[8] This
raised the question whether the Reagan administration
intended the deployment of Pershing II and cruise
missiles as a stop-gap measure -- similar to the
decision of the Eisenhower administration to deploy Thor
and Jupiter missiles in the 1950s -- until the perceived
weaknesses in the American intercontinental strategic
arsenal could be redressed in the late 1980s.[9]

All this called into question Washington's readiness
to bargain away the deployment of Pershing IIs and
cruise missiles in Western Europe, or, at the very
least, exposed its failure to exploit the leverage that
the deployment provided for the US negotiating stance in
Geneva. Moreover, the Reagan administration's anti-
Soviet rhetoric and its black-and-white view of the
East-West contest called into question the substance as
well as style of American diplomacy. One of the heaviest
burdens placed upon the transatlantic alliance was the
failure of the Reagan administration to develop an
attitude (not to speak of a policy) toward the Soviet
Union that would have conveyed anything by confron-
tational hostility.[10] Characterizing the Soviet Union as
an "evil empire" and elevating the contest between West
and East to a crusade between the forces of light and
darkness elicited among Europeans not only ridicule but
also the fear that this Manichaen struggle would be
decided on their own territory. As a consequence, the
West Europeans were determined to compensate for the

lack of a constructive American policy with one of their
own, with the somewhat ironic result that the nations
closest to the Soviet threat -- in Central and Western
Europe -- appeared more confident than their distant and
secure transatlantic partner of being able to deal with
it through diplomatic and political means. All this
brought into sharp focus the central paradox in the West
Europeans' attitude toward their nuclear protector: they
seem to be equally afraid that the United States will
use nuclear weapons, or that it will not. They fear, in
equal measure, lack of American circumspection and lack
of American resolve; they worry about the global
confrontation with the Soviet Union that Washington
seems to favor, but they also fear the possibility of
American neo-isolationism and disengagement from Europe.
Were it not for the fact that the Soviet Union, for its
part, has been unable to fashion a sophisticated
European policy -- above all, in its apparent inability
to define its security in terms other than military --
the transatlantic connection would be even weaker than
it already is.

Most fundamentally perhaps, the euro-missile
controversy demonstrated that there is no longer
agreement among the Western powers over the nature and
intensity of the Soviet threat. In part, no doubt, these
differing assessments derived from the differing views
provided by a global and by a regional geo-political
perspective: Washington sees itself challenged by Moscow
everywhere and on everything, the Europeans take a
narrower and more limited view of the Soviet threat. But
there are reasons for the differing views of the Soviet
Union that cannot be explained by global and regional
perspectives alone. American policy-makers, especially
in the current administration, tend to see the global
contest as a zero-sum game between the United States and
the Soviet Union where one's loss is the other's
immediate and automatic gain; they fail to comprehend
that the political and psycholological distance that
some Europeans wish to place between themselves and
Washington does not, for that reason, move them closer
to Moscow. The perjorative metaphor of "equidistance,"
with its implication that the European's reservations
about American diplomacy place them at one corner of an
equilateral political and moral triangle, is totally
misleading. Over the last two decades or so, many
Europeans have become apprehensive about what they
consider America's mismanagement of domestic as well as
foreign affairs, and they have developed -- along with
their own increasing self-assurance -- a more guarded
view of their transatlantic partner. This does not mean
they are "neutralist" or "anti-American," but it does
mean that the confidence in American diplomacy that
Washington seeks to sustain among its allies must be
continually earned in the day-to-day conduct of American

foreign policy. It has to be earned as well in the conduct of American domestic policy, for many Europeans connect their view of Washington's foreign policy with their assessment of the political reliability and circumspection of their transatlantic partner, evolving as much from their perception of America's future domestic political order as from their perception of current American diplomacy.

For a variety of complicated reasons, it has become more difficult to persuade America's West European allies to follow uncritically the security guidelines promulgated by the alliance superpower. Many West Germans, although convinced that German security interest required the Federal Republic's continuing support of NATO, were not eager to see additional nuclear weapons installed on their territory: relative to its size, the Federal Republic already contained more nuclear weapons than any country in the world; and the anticipated deployment of new intermediate range nuclear weapons was perceived as a major threat by the Soviet Union and thus increased East-West tensions.

The Germans' unease was not limited to the left wing of the political spectrum (although it was most pronounced there, including the left wing of the Social Democratic Party); and considering the wide-spread disenchantment in Europe with American diplomacy -- a disenchantment that begins to encompass what Europeans consider the unpredictable vagaries of American domestic politics -- it should not be surprising that it finds expression in shrill as well as in measured tones. Some elements of the German peace movement, in particular, nurture an anti-American bias -- a bias that is also noticeable among some members of the so-called Green Party, which obtained small representation in the German Bundestag following the March 1983 elections. But the peace movement and the heterogeneously constituted "Greens," whose political platform includes nuclear as well as environmental, practical as well as metaphysical concerns, will have less of a long-range impact on German-American relations than the intricate and difficult issue of the so-called "successor generation."[11] Germans under the age of forty have few recollections of American diplomacy in the postwar period and of the remarkable rapport that developed between American and German policy makers in the late 1940s and throughout the 1950s. Military victories are always harsh on the vanquished. But American military victory over Germany at the end of World War II was soon followed by a more gentle and leisurely conquest, accomplished by economic inducements, political prodding and diplomatic persuasion. It is not necessary to speculate about the precise mix of purposes that motivated American diplomacy -- altruistic considerations, enlightened self-interest, hegemonic aspirations, or the determination to enlist the Germans as allies against the Soviet Union -- the fact remains that in those years the foundations were laid for a remarkably stable German-American relationship that was to obtain, in both countries, a solid measure of bipartisan domestic political support. The infiltration of Western Europe by the transatlantic imperial power, accomplished through the benevolent and irresistable invasions of the American economy and the American way of life, established for the United States a sphere of influence every bit as pervasive as the one that the Red Army secured for the Soviet Union and Eastern Europe.

This was especially important for the Federal Republic. In the 1950s, the West Germans, in contrast to their East German compatriots, became persuaded that their superpower protector showed them the way toward poltical, economic and perhaps even moral rehabilitation. There existed, in the formative stage of the Federal Republic's development, a striking correspondence between the principles of the international economic order guided by the United States and supplemented by the institutions of West European integration. The German penchant for low inflation rates, budgetary discipline, and trade liberalization was reciprocated by the United States; the Bretton Woods monetary regime came to full implementation in the late 1950s with the free convertibility of currencies, ushering in a period of equilibrium between past dollar shortages and future dollar gluts; and such ventures as the Schuman Plan and the European Economic Community yielded Germany political as well as economic gains. In addition, Washington and Bonn's attitudes on how to contain the Soviet Union, as well as the personality traits of German and American leaders, were more congenial than at any time thereafter.

The generation of Germans that reached some measure of political awareness in the 1960s and 1970s is informed by a significantly different image of the United States. Vietnam and Watergate, American sponsorship of oligarchic regimes, and a variety of other questionable attitudes and practices that appear to align American diplomacy almost inevitably with entrenched rather than reform-minded interests have created a much less benevolent image of the United States than the one projected in earlier decades. Again, this change in perception of the United States does not, for that reason, imply a compensatory German or West European sympathy for the Soviet Union: our allies expect more of the United States than from the Soviet Union and -- after all -- we expect them to expect more. But most importantly perhaps, beyond the question of image, appearance, and the inevitable value changes that are associated with "generation gaps," there came about a new reality: as the international balance of power

began to shift in the 1970s, it became apparent that
across a wide array of issues -- economic, monetary,
military-strategic and political -- German and American
interests simply were no longer as congruent as they had
been in earlier decades. There is a broad and deep
reservoir of good will toward the United States in the
Federal Republic that stretches across the incremental
and porous boundaries of age, socio-economic status, or
political awareness. But the translation of that good
will into the practical policies that ultimately
determine the nature of German-American relations does
not proceed automatically, but requires circumspection
and nurturing on both sides of the Atlantic --
especially on security matters that are perceived to be
central to the respective national interests.

Seen against the broader context of German attitudes
on the East-West contest, on their geographical and
historical emplacement on the continent, and on their
relationship with the United States, the issues of the
eurostrategic military balance -- important as it is in
its own right -- takes on a meaning that goes far beyond
its military-technical import and extends into
fundamental questions about the future shape of the
transatlantic alliance and the European political order.
German attitudes are formed, or hardened, on the issue
of the eurostrategic nuclear balance in a way that will
reverberate and extend into adjacent issues of
German-American relations and affect them for years to
come. The highly technical discussions over arms control
measures, and the highly emotional response that these
discussions can evoke, are both related to fundamental
political attitudes (in West Germany as well as in the
United States) about the nature of the East-West
conflict and the shape of a desirable regional and
global world order. As security issues have reemerged as
major concerns in German-American relations, it is
essential to realize that these concerns, even more so
than in the 1960s, reflect and portend political
purposes that go far deeper than weighing the regional
or global military balance or redefining the meaning of
security for the 1980s and beyond. The context of
defense policy and arms control issues is large --
chronologically, geographically, and politically -- and
many of the problems raised by these issues are
technical, intricate and intractable. They are technical
because the technology of opposing weapons systems is
complex and dynamic and not amenable to clear-cut,
one-to-one comparisons: a balanced view of East-West
capabilities in Europe requires both quantative and
qualitative considerations. The problems are intricate
because the asymmetry of weapons is compounded by
asymmetries of purpose, geography, historical
experience, political will, moral restraint, use of
strategic doctrine, and many others. Finally, many of

the problems appear intractable because the limits which
define mutually acceptable arms control arrangements are
the same limits that define political accommodation.
When these limits are insufficiently flexible, neither
political purpose nor arms control can be realized or
advanced. In Europe, the limits that define arms control
are at the same time the boundaries that contain the
possibilities for the evolution of a new European order.

NOTES

1. For an analysis of the fluctuations of US
national security policies, see John Lewis Gaddis,
Strategies of Containment: A Critical Appraisal of
Postwar American National Security Policy (New York:
Oxford University Press, 1982). As early as 1965,
Franz-Josef Strauss argued that European doubts about
whether the United States could be relied upon "to
incinerate themselves in a nuclear holocaust for the
sake of Europe's freedom" were enhanced by "the frequent
changes in American strategic doctrines ... We have had
the Radford Doctrine, which was a modified John Foster
Dulles Doctrine. We have witnessed the introduction of
nuclear weapons into the alliance by giving the Allies
the means of delivery for tactical nuclear weapons and
retaining control and custody in American hands. Then
came the McNamara Doctrine, from counter-city strategy
to counter-force strategy, the theory of a pause on the
threshold, and now an increased trend back to massive
retaliation, not automatic as at the time of the Radford
Doctrine, but in the case of extended military
operations or to halt an aggressor when he has reached a
certain line." Franz-Josef Strauss, The Grand Design: A
European Solution to German Reunification (New York:
Praeger, 1966), p. 50.
2. Article VI of the North Atlantic Treaty, which
limits the geographical area of NATO to north of the
Tropic of Cancer, was initially pushed by the United
States to avoid NATO's entanglement in colonial wars.
Later, it was primarily the United States which called
for the enlargement of NATO's geographical area of
responsibility.
3. See Wolfram F. Hanrieder, The Stable Crisis: Two
Decades of German Foreign Policy (New York: Harper &
Row, 1970), ch.1.
4. For a discussion of the technical and political
issues raised by the "double-track" decision, see Marsha
McGraw-Olive and Jeffrey D. Porro, eds., Nuclear Weapons
in Europe: Modernization and Limitation (Lexington,

Mass.: Lexington Books, 1983); see also Wolfram F. Hanrieder, ed., Arms Control and Security: Current Issues (Boulder, Co.: Westview Press, 1979).
5. See McGeorge Bundy, George F. Kennan, Robert B. McNamara, and Gerard Smith, "Nuclear Weapons and the Atlantic Alliance," Foreign Affairs, Spring 1982. For a German response to Bundy, et.al., see Karl Kaiser, Georg Leber, Alois Mertes, and Franz-Joseph Schulze, "Nuclear Weapons and the Preservation of Peace," Foreign Affairs, Summer 1982.
6. Michael Howard, "Reassurance and Deterrence: Western Defense in the 1980s," Foreign Affairs, Winter 1982-83, p. 354.
7. See Hadley Bull, "European Self-Reliance and the Reform of NATO," Foreign Affairs, Spring 1983.
8. Projected initial operational capability (IOC) for the weapons systems involved in the US strategic force modernization program, assuming full funding, are as follows:

Advanced B-1B-IOC September, 1986; Full Capacity June, 1988;
Stealth Bomber -- IOC early 1990s;
Midgetman -- IOC 1989 in some modes;
Trident II (D-5) with Mark 500 Evader warhead -- IOC FY 1989
see, Aviation Week and Space Technology, March 14, 1983, pp. 23-31.
9. For a fuller exploration of this dimension, see Wolfram F. Hanrieder, Fragmente der Macht: Die Aussenpolitik der Bundesrepublik (Munich: Piper, 1981), pp. 114-125.
10. The Reagan administration seems to entertain a view of the Soviet Union similar to the one Edmund Burke expressed about the French Revolution: "I never thought we could make peace with the /Jacobin/ system; because it was not for the sake of an object that we pursued in rivalry with each other, but with the system itself, that we were at war. As I understood the matter, we were at war not with its conduct, but with its existence; convinced that its existence and its hostility were the same." (Second Letter on a Regicide Peace).
11. For an extensive discussion of the issue, which includes public-opinion surveys, see Chapter Three in Stephen F. Szabo, ed. The Successor Generation: International Perspectives of Postwar Europeans (London: Butterworth & Co., 1983).

4. Soviet Foreign Policy from Crossroads to Crossroads

Vernon V. Aspaturian

Introduction

There is every reason to believe that the United States and the Soviet Union are on the brink of an important restructuring of their relations to one another and this reformation of their relationship cannot but inevitably leave its impact upon other states and regions, not the least of which is Western Europe. Although the historic shift in the world "correlation of forces" which Soviet leaders and writers have been prophesying for some time has not arrived, a shift that would irreversibly tilt the balance of power in favor of the Soviet orbit, the Soviet Union has achieved rough military parity with the United States and in some areas has threatened to surpass it. During the decade of the 1970s, the Soviet leadership took advantage of a concatenation of fortuitous events that enabled it to enhance and project its strategic power, expand and intervene in new areas of the world (particularly Africa), threaten China, intimidate Europe by upsetting the theater nuclear balance, support Vietnam's expansion, invade Afghanistan, encircle Iran, and reassert its presence and involvement in the Arab-Israeli conflict via its adoption of Syria as its main instrument and client state in the Eastern Mediterranean.

With the advent of the Reagan administration, the tempting low-risk international atmosphere of the Carter years gave way to a resurgence of rhetorical self-confidence, vitality and threat in Washington at a time when impending paralysis, indecision and demoralization pervaded Moscow as Brezhnev's colleagues awaited with anxiety death, irreversible debility, or removal from office and the uncertain course of a new struggle for power in the Soviet Union that would follow. Thus, Soviet-American relations stand before another important phase in their evolution since the end of World War II, one that will be as equally significant as the stage which was set into motion by the successful

Soviet invasion of Czechoslovakia and the American
debacle in Vietnam.

Just as the Tet offensive and the anti-War movement
in the United States demoralized and paralyzed President
Johnson, sowed the seeds of doubt concerning America's
role and direction in world affairs, and fractured the
post-war foreign policy consensus in the United States,
the successful invasion of Czechoslovakia executed at
about the same time invigorated an indecisive Soviet
leadership, whose self-confidence and self-assurance
continued to wax as that of successive American
administrations waned during the seventies. The
simultaneous occurence of these events altered the
political, military and psychological balance and set
the stage for SALT I and the decade of détente that
ensued.

And just as the resurgence of Soviet self-assurance
and assertiveness came at an unfortunate time for the
United States in 1968-69, the recrudescence of American
vigor and resolve at the beginning of the eighties comes
at an awkward time for the new Soviet leadership. The
juxtaposition of events in 1968-69 created the
foundation for SALT I and the decade of détente; the new
configuration of events promises to create the basis for
a new stage in the evolution of Soviet-American
relations.

From the perspective of the Soviet leadership, the
decade of "easy pickings" is over, and while the early
rhetorical aggressiveness of President Reagan and
Secretaries Haig and Weinberger may have been
controversial and even excessive, it apparently has
convinced the Soviet leadership that this is an
administration determined to reassert American resolve
and restore America's eroding military power. If not in
pursuit of absolute or relative military superiority, in
the view of Moscow, the Reagan administration is at
least ready to halt the erosion of the strategic balance
at the center and prepared to redress the imbalances at
its margins.

The military parity between the United States and
the Soviet Union that was institutionalized by SALT I in
1972 was clearly recognized, but never publicly stated,
by the Soviet leadership as artificial, contrived and
ascriptive in character. SALT I reflected an agreement
between the world's only authentic mature global power,
temporarily debilitated and disoriented by internal
political convulsions, and an emergent global power,
whose only approximation to parity with the United
States was in the military realm. The Soviet leadership
appreciated both the evanescent nature of the existing
military balance (given the economic and technological
potential of the USA), and the temporary "window of
opportunity" if not vulnerability it afforded the Soviet
Union in world affairs.

The Soviet Union was a global power, but not an equal global power, since its inferiority to the United States economically, technologically, scientifically, in its quality of life, standard of living, system resilience and stability, was so painfully and humiliatingly evident. The Soviet leadership renounced all pretense at catching up with the United States in these various dimensions, and decided to concentrate its efforts and resources towards the development of its military power. The Soviet leadership thus realizes that its vaunted parity with the United States is still substantially asymmetrical and to a certain extent still artificial, since it also depends upon the continuing self-restraint of the United States and the Western powers, especially the two economic giants, West Germany and Japan. Should the Western powers be impelled or induced to devote a share of their substantial resources and capabilities to defense, even only approximately proportionate to that diverted by the Soviet Union, the relative military power and influence ot the Soviet Union would be radically diminished. The Soviet leaders are cognizant of this potential, and while they correctly calculate that for political and other reasons, the Western powers are unlikely to match the Soviet effort proportionately, their policies and behavior will be designed to ensure that this continues. The appearance and rise of the anti-nuclear and peace movements in Western Europe and the United States are perceived by the Soviet leaders as important internal restraining mechanisms and they give them consistent if unsolicited and unwelcome support, whereas the repeated Soviet disavowal of seeking military or strategic superiority since 1977 is designed to rhetorically diminish the impact of the massive Soviet military buildup of the seventies.

The Soviets have learned, as others have throughout history, that whereas military power is not a precise surrogate for economic and other kinds of power, or vice versa, military power can promise quick and tangible short-term dividends that may powerfully influence the shaping of the long-term future, and depending upon the degree of resolve and ruthlessness, military power can also be a productive economic investment. In this connection, it would not be inappropriate to mention the appearance of a new book by Soviet Foreign Minister and Politburo member Andrei Gromyko entitled, The External Expansion of Capital in History and the Present. Its main thesis is that Western capiatalism used its superior power to enrich itself at the expense of weaker areas of the world, and in the words of a favorable reviewer in the person of Georgi Arbatov, proposed that the Soviet Union "must propose a positive alternative to it/i.e. Western exploitation/ and find ways of internationalizing production and forms of the

international division of labor that would neither
encroach on the sovereignty of states nor 'export'
exploitation,"[1] which suspiciously sounds as if the
Soviet Union is ready to make a greater demand and claim
on the resources of the globe and to develop the means
to implement them.

At some point after SALT II, therefore, although the
Soviet leadership publicly stated that rough military
parity existed (in the view of some observers, Moscow
was actually allowed a certain margin of quantitative
superiority), the Soviet leadership made the important
decision to maintain a high level of military
expenditures at the expense of imbalancing the entire
Soviet economy. This high rate of military spending was
sustained through the decade even as economic growth
declined. The heavy cost of mortgaging the economy in
order to exploit political and diplomatic opportunities
in the world at large, created by the temporary American
retrenchment, and frustrated Soviet expectations,
probably accounts for much of the bitter resentment
directed at the Reagan Administration, whose hard-line
reassertiveness in foreign and military policy threatens
to nullify whatever advantages Moscow hoped to exploit
and gain. It appears that a controversy may have been
unleashed within the Soviet leadership as to whether the
political harvest was worth the short and long-term
costs to Soviet society and damage to the Soviet
economy. Thus, one of the awkward paradoxes of the
Soviet scene as it confronts the Reagan Administration
-- a relatively ravaged economic and a flourishing
Soviet military establishment -- has grave implications
for the future of Soviet-American relations and the
internal politics of the Soviet Union that are both
ambiguous and ominous. This point will be amplified
below.

There appears to be some evidence to suggest that
the initial hard-line rhetoric of the Reagan
administration was responsible, at least in part, for
blunting the Soviet momentum in foreign policy, although
the uncertainty concerning Brezhnev's successors may
have also contributed to the evident low-keyed character
of Soviet behavior during the past two years. Reagan's
resolute rhetoric, his handling of the air controllers'
strike, his ambiguous allusions to limited nuclear war,
while frightening sectors of the American and West
European public, may have simultaneously had a dampening
effect upon the cautious, unenergetic old men in the
Kremlin as well. Since much of the early harsh rhetoric
was directed at Cuba, the Sandanistas, and their support
of the guerillas in El Salvador, it was not surprising
that Castro publicly took this rhetoric seriously and
obliquely conceded that it had served to moderate his
own behavior in order to avoid provoking the Reagan

administration or providing it with any conceivable
pretext to take direct action against Havana.
In this connection, it might be tempting to suggest
that the harsh rhetoric may have made the margin of
difference in dissuading the Soviets from invading
Poland, in deterring an escalation of the war in
Afghanistan, and even in influencing Andropov to accept
in principle a lower number of SS-20s in Europe than are
currently deployed. This, of course cannot be proven
since, by logic and definition, no valid empirical test
of an effective deterrence is possible. Deterrence is
successful only if nothing happens, and if nothing
happens, it becomes impossible to prove that various
policies, gestures, or actions were responsible for the
non-happening.

Current Conditioning Factors
A survey and inventory of existing conditioning
factors that may influence and shape the configuration
of a restructured relationship between the United States
and the USSR would be in order at this point. It will
quickly become evident as these conditioning factors are
examined, that they do not all move in the same
direction; and that, in fact, they generate ambivalent,
ambiguous and, at this point, still uncertain trends and
tendencies. Some of these factors work to the advantage
of the United States and Western Europe, others to the
advantage of the Soviet Union, and still others are
mixed in their impact and unpredictable in their
efforts, since a number of equally plausible, but not
necessarily compatible or consistent, directions are
possible. In other words, cross-currents and other
inconsistent and incompatible trends will be generated
by these conditioning factors, and their resolution or
accommodation will influence the shape of whatever new
equilibrium emerges.
The most important conditioning factor, and one to
which the current administration has not entirely
adjusted, and to which the Carter Administration may
have over-accomodated is the emergence of the Soviet
Union as an authentic global power, a condition which is
not immediately susceptible to reversal. Achieving this
status was the single most important achievement of the
Brezhnev era and rests almost entirely upon the military
power accumulated by Moscow during the past decade. As
noted earlier, it has paid dearly for this military
achievement, and its pay-off has yet to equal the cost.
The current Soviet leadership is not likely to enter
into any relationship that might threaten this status
and its collateral claim to equality with the United
States in the international system. Brezhnev and his
military commanders made this quite clear and Andropov
and Ustinov have repeatedly restated this position. And
while the Soviet leadership probably recognizes that the

era of the post Vietnam/Watergate period and its opportunities are also not likely to reappear in the proximate future, it is equally clear that the days of American superiority will not be restored either. The situation appears ripe, from both perspectives, for a renewed normalized and stable relationship, based upon a new equilibrium.

A second conditioning factor is the transformation of the psychological balance brought about by the Soviet achievement of military parity with the United States at the strategic and global level. For the first time in its history, the Soviet Union has achieved near-invulnerability to attack, a condition which is diametrically at variance with the almost continuous exposure to attack that characterized the Soviet and Russian historical past, a vulnerability that has so powerfully shaped Russia's strategic culture and its susceptibility to paranoia and suspicion.

At the same time, the United States has, for the first time in its recent history, lost its near absolute invulnerability to direct devastating assault. To be sure, the United States today is no less vulnerable or invulnerable than the Soviet Union as a result, but the psychological direction from which each has approached this condition of mutually equal vulnerability or invulnerability is different. The Soviet Union, whose past history has been one of continuous vulnerability to attack from various directions, has now achieved near invulnerability, whereas the United States, whose past history has been one of absolute invulnerability, now finds itself in the uncomfortable position of being subject to direct devastating attack. It is the direction from which each country comes to this condition of mutually equal invulnerability that accounts for the change in the psychological balance.

Nuclear weapons, for the United States, until recently, were essentially instruments designed to deter and contain Soviet expansion rather than to directly protect the United States, whereas for the Soviet Union, nuclear weapons emerge as a liberating shield, freeing it from its previous vulnerability to attack and containment. Thus, nuclear weapons serve as essentially a positive force from the Soviet perspective whereas they are essentially still perceived as a negative or restraining instrument from the American perspective. Because nuclear weapons and the equality they impart to the Soviet Union are more salient in defining the Soviet role and position in the international community than the American, no agreement with the Soviet Union is likely that will diminish this status. Not only does Soviet equality with the United States rest almost entirely upon its nuclear military prowess, but Moscow's status in relation to third parties is also defined by its military capabilities. That is why nuclear reduction

agreements limited only to the United States and the
Soviet Union on the size and configuration of their
respective nuclear capabilities are likely to be
unsatisfactory. It also explains the seemingly
unreasonable attitude of Moscow's toward the British and
French nuclear forces. But, above all, lurking behind
the shadows is China and its nuclear capability.

Any reduction in the absolute strategic capabilities
of the two global powers automatically enhances the
relative nuclear strength of France, Britain and China.
For China in particular, any reduction in Soviet
strategic capability is tantamount to an increase in
Chinese capability vis-à-vis the Soviet Union. It is the
simultaneous growth in both relative and absolute power
that has created the symbiosis rendering the Soviet
Union nearly invulnerable to attack from any direction.
This does not mean that the military power of the Soviet
Union is greater than that of all its potential
adversaries combined, or even greater than that of the
USA alone, but rather that the margin of difference at
this juncture has reached the point of near
invulnerability for the Soviet Union at the expense of
greater vulnerability for China, Japan, Western Europe
and the United States.

And, indeed, the next stage in the developing
nuclear momentum of the Soviet Union appeared designed
to render its potential adversaries increasingly
vulnerable to Soviet pressure and intimidation, not
simply as an adjunct to increasing Soviet security, but
also to convert a costly military investment into a
profitable political and eventually profitable economic
investment. In its rationale for introducing the SS-20s
into Europe and the Far East, Moscow has implicitly
demanded as a matter of right that its nuclear
capability be equal to that of all other nuclear powers
combined, which would simultaneously legitimize nuclear
superiority over the United States. This is essentially
an extension of the Soviet justification for quantitative superiority advanced at the time of SALT I when
the existence of a separate Chinese nuclear threat was
invoked. Having been successful in extracting, in
effect, an additional "Chinese increment" in 1972,
Andropov, just as Brezhnev before him, insisted upon an
additional "Franco-British increment" at the sub-
strategic level. This, of course, should be resisted;
the price of success-rejection may be, however, an
ultimate merging of negotiations at the strategic and
sub-strategic levels with the inclusion of Britain,
France and China as formal participants to any
agreement. At the same time, the Soviet Union appears to
be opposed to broadening participation in nuclear
negotiations for fear of undermining its position as the
only equal to the United States.

In general, the condition of mutually equal invulnerability/vulnerability has probably served to make the Soviets more confident, assured and optimistic, and the Americans less confident and more pessimistic because of the psychological direction of movement towards this condition. But this has been somewhat mitigated by other factors, most notably the change in leadership in both the United States and the Soviet Union, which will be discussed below.

At this point it might be useful to deal with the issue of Soviet strategic culture and the degree to which its conceptions of defense and security must be accommodated. Because of past Soviet and Russian vulnerability, the traditional Russian approach to security has been to increase the vulnerability and insecurity of its potential enemies. This has usually involved a mixture of political-diplomatic duplicity, pervasive secrecy and suspicion, and massive quantities of weapons and troops to make up for a deficiency in quality. These are difficult behavioral patterns and habits to renounce and Leninist doctrine has served to reenforce rather than to abandon them. The result has been national collective paranoia, which has been the familiar topic of many observers.

Aside from the fact that no state is obligated to accept is own vulnerability and insecurity as a condition for Russian/Soviet security, the current state of Soviet military power and the near invulnerability it has imparted to the Soviet Union renders an accommodation to Soviet paranoia somewhat moot and can no longer be reasonably invoked as a justification or apology for Soviet behavior and policies, which some analysts continue to do. Neither the United States nor Western Europe (China certainly will not) should allow itself to be maneuvered into accepting the proposition that, given the traditional Russian/Soviet paranoia and sense of insecurity stemming from its past history, and given the parameters of its strategic culture, the US and Western Europe should accept the risk of a certain degree of unilateral vulnerability in order to reassure the Soviet leadership and maximize the prospects of agreement on arms control.

The Western position on vulnerability has always been in principle, and should so remain, that as long as vulnerability remains a principal criterion or reference point in calculating the strategic equation, it must be both mutual and equal. This is a concept with which the Soviet leaders are uncomfortable, not only because of past experience, but also because mutual and equal vulnerability translates into mutual and equal deterrence, a condition which the Soviet leaders also find uncongenial. Most observers tend to stress the mutuality of deterrence and neglect the condition of

equality, or assume that equality is encompassed by the
concept of mutuality.
     This is not the case. Whereas Soviet leaders have
tended to find mutual deterrence tolerable if not
exactly acceptable, they reject the concept of equal or
symmetrical deterrence as an acceptable Soviet normative
objective. From the Soviet perspective, mutual and
symmetrical deterrence would mean accepting the status
quo, to which they have repeatedly stated they are
opposed. Indeed, the USSR explicitly seeks to change the
status quo, and its spokesmen ruminate periodically
about the need to restructure the international system
and consistently reiterate their commitment to a
universal socialist order. To accept mutual and
symmetrical (i.e. equal) deterrence, from the Soviet
point of view, would be tantamount to accepting
"self-containment." On more than one occasion, and in
the presence of Western leaders, Soviet leaders have
insisted that history has ordained the imperative of
change in a certain predetermined direction and that
neither détente nor peaceful co-existence can or should
be interpreted as a Soviet commitment to refrain from
encouraging revolution to say nothing of opposing it.
     This ideological imperative has been increasingly
linked to Soviet conceptions of defense and security and
is defined as military obligation. Thus, in 1974, the
former Soviet Defense Minister, Marshal A.A. Grechko,
said:

> At the present stage, the historic function of the
> Soviet Armed Forces is not restricted to their
> function in defending our Motherland and the other
> socialist countries. In its foreign policy activity
> the Soviet state purposefully opposes the export of
> counterrevolution and the policy of oppression,
> supports the national liberation struggle, and
> resolutely resists imperialists' aggression in
> whatever distant region of our planet it may
> appear.[2]

     Thus, the Soviet leadership perceives as part of its
defense function the deterrence of the "export of
counter revolution," while it seeks to preserve the
unilateral right to avoid the deterrence of its support
for "national liberation movements" (i.e., the "export
of revolution") which under any rubric is a demand for
an asymmetrical deterrence in its favor.
     These obligations have now been enshrined in the new
1977 constitution and thus have been converted from
ideological commitments into state obligations. In an
entirely new chapter on foreign policy, the 1977 Soviet
constitution, under Article 28, defines the goals of
Soviet foreign policy as follows:

The foreign policy of the USSR is aimed at ensuring international conditions favorable for building communism in the USSR, safeguarding the state interests of the Soviet Union, consolidating the positions of world socialism, supporting the struggle of peoples for national liberation and social progress, preventing wars of aggression, achieving universal and complete disarmament, and consistently implementing the principle of peaceful coexistence of states with different social systems.[3]

It would be reasonable to assume that the seven distinct goals of Soviet foreign policy as enumerated in Article 28 are listed in order of priority and precedence, in which case the support of national liberation movements has a conspicuously higher priority than either arms control or peaceful co-existence, a matter of no small importance that has serious implications in terms of defining the parameters of future arms control agreements that are acceptable to the Soviet Union.

And more recently the links between ideology, prestige, greater power status and security were articulated in even more graphic language. In an interview with Joseph Kraft, the influential Soviet journalist Alexander Bovin, in response to a Kraft query as to whether Russia would collapse if Poland were allowed a greater latitude of internal political autonomy, gave a concrete meaning to the words "consolidating the positions of world socialism":

"It is not a matter of our physical security...It is a matter of relations between a great power and smaller states that are socialist states. Not only security is at stake but ideology as well. For example, if Lech Walesa became the leader of Poland, Poland would leave the Warsaw Pact. That would not be a threat to our physical security, but it would be a terrible loss of prestige. It would be like what happened to you in Iran. When the United States was thrown out of Iran, the United States lost prestige everywhere."[4]

The Soviet leadership has tended to accept mutual deterrence at the strategic level, since the likely alternative is a mutually catastrophic nuclear war. There is little question but that the Soviet leadership has one of its highest priorities in the avoidance of nuclear war, but not at the expense of abandoning Soviet ideological and system expansion if at all possible. Thus, Moscow continues to resist mutual deterrence at levels below the strategic, and insists upon asymmetrical deterrence whereby it seeks to deter at those levels without being deterred in turn. This explains why the Soviet leaders have consistently rejected "linkage," which they read to mean a unilateral American attempt to impose upon the Soviet Union mutual deterrence at substrategic levels in return for an American acceptance of mutual deterrence at the strategic level. From the Soviet perspective, this emerges essentially as a variant of the traditional American containment policy whereby the Soviet Union voluntarily accepts constraints upon the further expansion of its power and system.

The linkage that exists between equality with the United States, global power status, quantitative and qualitative levels of nuclear capability, and security defined in terms of approximation to invulnerability, that exists in Soviet calculations must be closely examined in order to anticipate Soviet reactions to various kinds of arms control proposals. Equality, status, level, and security are four separable but interlocked factors and the implications of their interrelationship are not always clearly amplified. Thus, in the Soviet perspective, the key variable which will determine global power status and security is not equality with the United States, but rather the quantitative and qualitative level of nuclear capability. Equality with the US, at too low a level would endanger both Moscow's global power status and security, but not necessarily affect the United States to the same degree. The absolute level of nuclear power for the United States is salient only to the extent that it is related to the level of Soviet nuclear capability, whereas for Moscow both equality with the US and the absolute level at which equality is sustained are salient.

Thus the centrality of the Soviet Union's obsession with its self-perception as a global power equal to the United States and its incidental intolerance for competitors of a similar aspiration poses a crucial problem for the long-range solution of arms contol. China rejects what she condemns as super-power hegemony, although she can do little about it for the moment, and refuses to accept the quasi-legitimate duopoly of the US and the USSR on global power status. In particular, China resents and rejects the Soviet claim to that role as both unwarranted and pretentious, which probably reflects the contempt which the Chinese have for the standards and values of Soviet-Russian culture and achievements. For the Soviet Union, on the other hand, its current nuclear capability and the near impregnability it has conferred are irretrievably linked to Moscow's self-identity as a global power, whose only equal is the United States. Any proposal that would result in a substantial diminution of Soviet nuclear power, even if an equal American reduction were involved, is likely to be unacceptable, since a deep reduction in Soviet nuclear power is likely to be perceived as an erosion of the special status Moscow has acquired.

Equality with the United States is, as noted earlier, only one variable in the Soviet nuclear calculation; a second calculation is the level at which equality exists, since it is the size of the gap between the nuclear power of the two global powers and the lesser nuclear powers that sets the two global powers apart, and a lowering of the level at which equality with the United States exists could seriously undermine the status of the Soviet Union as a global power without endangering the similar status of the United States. After all, the United States was a global power at lower levels of nuclear capability, whereas the Soviet Union became a global power only after certain levels of military capability were attained. Even if nuclear weapons did not exist, the United States could maintain its preeminent world status, whereas the Soviet Union without nuclear weapons would simply be another major power. Extending the illustration ever further, in a world without weapons at all, the Soviet Union's role would even be diminished below that of the major Western powers and Japan.

Thus proposals involving deep reductions in total number of launchers and warheads, or even proposals which would thin out Soviet capability (replacement of MIRVS with single-headed ICBMs), must be examined not only in terms of Soviet-American equality, but in what impact they will have on the status of Moscow vis-à-vis other nuclear powers. It is difficult to precisely calibrate at which point in the critical mass of nuclear weaponry the Soviet Union will suffer an erosion of its global power status. But apparently such a calculation exists in the minds of the Soviet leadership, but one that may be more intuitive than quantitative in character. An aspect of this intuitive calculation is a highly possible Soviet conviction that a measurable quantitative superiority in military power for the Soviet Union is necessary in order to maintain its status as an equal global power in order to compensate for its deficiencies in the non-military elements of national power.

All sorts of other explanations will be advanced in rejecting such proposals, but the underlying and determining reasons for rejection will remain Moscow's fear of losing its global power position and the opportunity for primacy that it offers.

It is this symmetrical and almost abnormal dependency upon military power for Moscow's international status and influence that will make it extremely difficult, if not impossible, to rid the world of nuclear weapons, or even to reduce them to a substantial degree, unless the Soviet leadership can be convinced that an even more unacceptable alternative can be imposed upon it.

This does not mean that a renewed relaxation of tensions between the two powers cannot take place; it can, but will have to take place within the context of essentially existing nuclear parameters, with the possibility even of continued expansion of nuclear capabilities by all nuclear powers. Agreements which credibly disaggregate intent from capability are about the best that can be expected under existing circumstances.

In assessing Soviet perceptions of how arms control will affect Moscow's security, status and opportunities -- for the latter are an important element in Soviet calculations -- it is insufficient and may even be disorienting to examine the results and process at each level of the military balance in isolation. Although the compartmentalization of three separate sets of negotiations in three different locations, that were largely suspended in 1983, made it easier to deal with the overall problem logistically and maximized the possibility of agreement in one arena or another, it also served to provide Moscow with a definite advantage. The Soviet leadership has carefully coordinated and monitored all three sets of negotiations to ensure compatibility and to minimize inconsistencies that may inadvertently result without careful and continuous cross-checking of the process and results.

In the three sets of negotiations, for all practical purposes, there was only a single negotiator on the Soviet side, whereas, even at the highest level, the START negotiations -- although the United States is the only formal Western party -- in fact considerable informal involvement by American allies had taken place. In the other two arenas, the Western side is multiple in character and requires the previous consensus of the parties and the ability to sustain that consensus over time and through changes in public mood and government. This is not always an easy thing to do, but as the INF negotiations demonstrate, it allows the Soviet Union considerable latitude to sow mischief and to maneuver and manipulate among the three sets of negotiations. Hence, the United States and its partners must be exceedingly careful to avoid being whiplashed among the three sets of negotiations in which Moscow seeks to recover in one arena that which it conceded in another. This is particularly the case in the gray area between the strategic and sub-strategic levels where weapons systems are deliberately designed to just barely avoid being counted as strategic weapons (the Backfire Bomber) or whose theater ranges seem inordinately excessive and easily convertible for strategic purposes (the SS-20 cum SS-16). These are only the most conspicuous

illustrations, and the Soviet side will continue to
discover more ingenious methods of obeying the letter
while violating the spirit of various agreements because
of this compartmentalization.

Among the most enigmatic conditioning factors is one
whose impact on future Soviet-American and Soviet-West
European relations is both highly uncertain and
tantalizingly suggestive -- the provisional character of
the current leadership succession process. Highly
significant changes have also taken place in the
leadership structures of the principal Western powers. A
strong conservative current has swept across Britain,
the United States and Western Germany during the waning
years of the Brezhnev era. Even in France, the socialist
Mitterand government has fallen into step with
surprising enthusiasm with an essentially conservative
position in dealing with the Soviet Union in strategic
and foreign policy issues. It is the Reagan
administration, out of step on trade and credit issues
with the major Western states, that has marred a
remarkable consensus on critical issues. On this point,
however, the Reagan administration appears to be moving
toward the West European position. Thus new leaderships
in the West, with new mandates supported by a different
array of domestic constituencies, will now face the
Chernenko coalition which also represents a new balance
of domestic Soviet constituencies, all of which promise
to produce an interesting if highly uncertain set of new
directions.

Of all the leadership changes, that in the Soviet
Union is the most critical for a number of reasons, only
some of which can be amplified upon here. The Soviet
leadership situation has been in a condition of flux and
uncertainty for several years, due to its aging
character. Within a matter of a few years, the five most
important members of the Soviet leadership that
succeeded Khrushchev have either been purged or died
(Brezhnev, Kosygin, Podgorny, Suslov, and Kirilenko),
and not a single full member of the Politburo that
succeeded Khrushchev is alive today. All of the
principal contenders to Brezhnev's power and authority
are relative new-comers to the Soviet apex. This
includes the three principal members of the dominant
coalition (Chernenko, Ustinov, and Gromyko). Since
Andropov's death and Chernenko's ascension to power, in
fact, the concentration of power has increased in the
hands of men who are even older than the deceased
erstwhile head of the KGB. Thus although the deaths of
Pelshe, Suslov, and Brezhnev and Kosygin, together with
the removal of Kirilenko -- all within the past five
years -- reduced the average age of the Politburo, all
of the major contenders are still nevertheless rather
advanced in age and in varying degrees of ill-health.
This also highlights another unique aspect of the

current Soviet leadership situation: the near
simultaneous death or removal of the five most important
leaders in the system (Kosygin, Andropov, Suslov,
Brezhnev, and Kirilenko). Currently, not a single full
member of the sitting Politburo was a full member at the
time of Khrushchev's ouster in 1964. Two full members,
Grishin and Shcherbitsky, were candidate members at the
time and in terms of service as full members are the
most senior in rank, having both been promoted to full
membership in 1971. Gromyko became a full member in
1973, Ustinov in 1975, while Chernenko and Tikhonov did
not become full members until 1978 and 1980
respectively. Thus, in terms of seniority, the dominant
coalition leaders are drawn from the middle levels of
seniority rather than from the senior or junior levels.
In terms of chronological age, however, as noted above,
it doesn't seem to make much difference.

Other precedents have also been broken. Until his
death, Andropov was the first Secretary General of the
Party that did not serve for a long period of time as a
senior secretary of the Central Committee (i.e., a
Secretary who is simultaneously a full member of the
Politburo). Andropov served as a senior secretary for
less than a year before Brezhnev's death, moving from
the KGB to the Secretariat after Suslov's death in order
to sanitize his credentials as a contender for the
succession, although he served for a time as a junior
secretary before his appointment to the KGB in 1967.

Andropov was the first Soviet leader to succeed to
the title of Secretary General, the highest position in
the system. Stalin converted the title into the highest
post; he abolished it in 1953. Khrushchev assumed the
more modest title of First Secretary. Brezhnev succeeded
to this title in 1964, reconverted it back to
Secretary-General in 1966, and institutionalized it as a
separate organ in 1971.

Another clue to the incomplete character of the
Soviet succession crisis is the uncertainty that
surrounds the post of Commander-in-Chief of the Armed
Forces. To date, it has not yet been revealed if
Chernenko also holds the position of Chairman of the
Council for Defense, a still shadowy but obviously
important decision-making organ. Even its current
membership has not been made public, although it appears
that Ustinov, Gromyko, Chernenko, and Tikhonov among
Politburo members are on this body, and that Marshals
Akhromeyev and Kulikov also serve on it in some
capacity.

Although the Defense Council is an organ
constitutionally created and presumably legally
subordinated to the Presidium of the Supreme Soviet and
its Chairman, in actual fact it apparently is supervised
by and reports to the Politburo. The Chairman of the
Defense Council can also serve as Supreme Commander-in-

Chief, but this is not automatic and is a separate
position, whose incumbency has not yet been publicly
revealed. In the past, it has not been unusual for the
post of Commander-in-Chief to remain vacant for long
periods of time (it was vacant at the time of the German
attack upon the Soviet Union in 1941 and the lack of a
stipulated Commander-in-Chief was responsible for the
aggravated character of early military reverses), or for
the appointment to be made by secret decree, which was
the case with respect to Khrushchev's assumption of the
title in 1956, which was not revealed until 1964.
Similarly Stalin was secretly appointed Commander-in-
Chief in July 1941, but this appointment was revealed
only after the Battle of Stalingrad in 1943.[5] In spite
of these precedents, the absence of a public
announcement concerning this position is another clue to
an unsettled situation.

As long as the Soviet succession process remains
unsettled, all Soviet policies and actions must be
closely examined and related to domestic controversies
and debates. Inevitably, Soviet initiatives, responses,
reactions, and other forms of Soviet behavior will be
shaped for their impact and influence at home as well as
abroad, in order not only to influence the behavior of
the outside world but also to influence the fortunes of
this or that poltical leader, faction or coalition
domestically. Even inertia, indecisiveness, paralysis,
and inconsistent pronouncements and actions may reflect
the domestic situation more than the external. It will
not always be easy to disaggregate actions designed for
internal effect as distinguished from those designed to
elicit reaction and responses from abroad. Just as
Soviet commentators charge that many Reagan proposals
are designed primarily for domestic effect or are a
result of internal political pressures, it can be
assumed that Soviet leaders labor under some Soviet
variant of the same vectoral pressures.

Other conditioning factors that can only be
mentioned at this point that will affect the future
restructuring of relations include the unbalanced
character of the Soviet economy and its various
debilities: declining growth rates, declining
productivity, labor shortages, corruption, inefficiency,
and incompetence of planners and managers, all of which
will have at least a marginal impact.

Still another conditioning factor, whose potential
impact is even more unclear, is the overextension of
Soviet involvements and commitments abroad, including
the different aspects of the Soviet variant of the
"burden of empire:" the war in Afghanistan, the
continuing ferment in Poland, with the underlying
tensions between the Polish military regime and the
ruling military-police-industrial coalition in the
Kremlin becoming more evident, the entanglements in

Ethiopia, Angola and Central America, and assorted
problems with other Communist countries, parties and
client states. Many of these obligations were assumed
during the Carter presidency, as part of the costs of
exploiting opportunities, but these burdens and risks
have now been increased by the higher-risk atmosphere
created by the Reagan administration.

The Outlook
    The interaction and impact of these various
conditioning factors upon Soviet policies and behavior
will be mixed, but on the whole they work towards a
period of Soviet moderation, consolidation, and
reexamination for the short term, i.e., the rest of this
decade. Short term policies and behavior for most of
this decade will be shaped by the continuing and
unraveling leadership succession process, which may no
longer be a simple raw struggle for power as in the
past, but more sophisticated, and constrained by the
experiences of the past and domestic "rules of the game"
that have progressively evolved. Since the Soviet
leaders will be primarily preoccupied with preserving
and improving their own positions, and given the age
structure of the Soviet leadership, we are likely in for
a period in which the actuarial imperatives will in
effect impose a succession of five or six year periods
of Soviet "administrations." Thus, by the time Chernenko
is ready to let go, die, or be forced from the scene at
about age 75, the next crop of successors, who are now
in their mid-sixties, will themselves be between 65 and
75 years old, and not good for much more than another
five years. This, of course, presupposes that neither
Chernenko nor whoever replaces him succeeds in
conducting a purge of the older members of the Politburo
and advancing younger people. Andropov's sudden
abandonment of his anti-corruption and anti-incompe-
tence campaign before his death suggests very strongly
that, coming as it did from a long-time Secret Police
Chief, this campaign was ominously and shudderingly
perceived by aging middle-level bureaucrats, against
whom it was aimed, as the threat of a purge, and all
that that implies within the context of the Soviet
scene.
    Currently, there are eleven full members of the
Politburo, four short of what was until recently a full
complement of fifteen. Only one new full member, Geidar
Aliyev, has been appointed during a period when four
full members died or were removed (Suslov, Brezhnev,
Kirilenko, and Pelshe). Since new appointments will
seriously affect alignments and the course of the
succession process, the character of new appointments or
lack of appointments will provide clues to the direction
of movement.

TABLE I

Age, Date of Appointment and Years of Service
of Full Politburo Members

Name	Birth Date	Age	Cand. Memb.	Full Memb.	Years as Full Memb.
Tikhonov	1905	78	1978	1980	3
Ustinov	1908	75	1965	1975	8
Gromyko	1909	74	--	1973	10
Chernenko	1911	72	1977	1978	5
Kunayev	1912	71	1966	1971	12
Grishin	1914	69	1961	1971	12
Sherbitsky	1918	65	1961	1971	12
Romanov	1923	60	1973	1976	7
Aliyev	1923	60	1976	1982	1
Gorbachev	1931	52	--	1979	4

In any event, the radical generational shift in
leadership which many Sovietologists anticipated has
been cleverly circumvented by the resourceful and shrewd
Soviet leaders who once again outwitted Western
prognosticators by resorting to ingenious and inherently
unpredictable measures: prolonging their life and
holding on to power. The generation gap disappeared
largely because the Brezhnev generation of leaders as a
group hung on to power for a sufficient period of time
to compensate for and bridge over the "lost generation."
This becomes quickly evident when we examine the age
structure of the current full members of the Politburo.
Since for the most part candidate members are selected
on the basis of different criteria (many are ex officio)
than full members, and tend to remain candidate members
until death or removal, they are not active participants
in the succession process (they have no vote in
decisions but can take part in discussions).

TABLE II

Date of Appointment, Years of Service and Age
at Time of Death or Removal of
Former Politburo Members

Name	Birth Date	Death Date	Age at Death or Removal	Cand. Membr.	Full Memb.	Years Full Memb.
Pelshe	1899	1983	84	--	1966	7
Suslov	1902	1981	79	1952	1955	28
Kirilenko	1906	1982	76	1957	1962	21
Brezhnev	1906	1982	76	1956	1957	26
Kosygin	1904	1980	76	1957	1960	23
Andropov	1914	1983	69	1967	1973	10

Thus, six members are over 70 years of age, one is between 65 and 70, while two are 61 and the youngest is 53. To place this group in overall appropriate generational perspective, the five members who died or were removed from membership since 1980 should also be noted.

When Table II is superimposed upon Table I, the strategy employed by Brezhnev and his associates, to make certain that radical traumatic generational shifts would not threaten the stability of the Soviet leadership, can be seen to be the recruitment of members to the Politburo who were largely in their own age group, rather than bringing in younger people from later generations. Thus Chernenko and Tikhonov were respectively 67 and 75 years of age when elevated to full membership. And thus, of the current eleven full members, no less than six are 70 years or older (roughly in the same generation as Brezhnev), but in terms of Politburo service, none has been a full member more than 12 years, with Tikhonov and Chernenko having only four and six years of service respectively.

Younger members have been appointed to the Politburo in the past, but their careers have been for the most part rather brief. Of the younger group, the youngest member, Gorbachev, was appointed at age 48 whereas Romanov was 52 and Aliyev 59 when appointed full members. Both had served as candidate members, however, with Romanov appointed a candidate member at age 50 and Aliyev at age 53.

All this suggests that the core of the Soviet leadership will continue to average 70 years or older for some time to come, barring any sudden reversal of past patterns or unprecedented internal or external crisis. (It will be interesting to see whether existing vacancies in the Politburo will be filled by cohorts of the senior members rather than younger blood.) This suggests that the age of the Soviet leadership will serve first to function as the chief constraint on the abuse of power in the Soviet system, since aging leaders will not have sufficient time to <u>consolidate</u> and <u>intensify</u> power; by the time they consolidate their power and establish their legitimacy, they will be ready to move on, to be succeeded once again by leaders or a leader whose incumbency is not likely to exceed six years. What constitutions and laws do for democratic political systems in terms of restraints and checks on the abuse, accumulation, and longevity of power, the actuarial imperatives accomplish as natural surrogates in the Soviet system. It will also serve to institutionalize authentic collective leadership.

An aging leadership also suggests caution and prudence in foreign affairs and aversion to adventurism and risk-taking, but at the same time, it works in favor of an experienced, mature and shrewd leadership that will continue to look out for opportunities to exploit and advantages to pursue. It will tend to hew to proven, demonstrated and familiar patterns of behavior, which probably means no radical reforms in the economic structure and no acceptance of arms control proposals which threaten radical surgery on the Soviet military. Above all, such a leadership will avoid the uncertain, the unfamiliar and the unsafe courses of action, whether in domestic or foreign policy.

The nature of any agreement reached with the United States, however, will be constrained by a number of limiting factors. As noted earlier, it is unlikely that any Soviet leader can or will enter into any agreement calling for a substantial reduction in Soviet strategic power, certainly not much beyond the crude and vague 25 per cent cut proposed earlier. At the INF level, the Reagan administration cannot retreat too much further from its current demand for US/USSR equality in deployed intermediate range nuclear missiles in Europe. The quantitative difference between Andropov's latest proposal and the President's demand for equality still allows sufficient latitude for a possible agreement. The sticking points are likely to be whether Moscow can successfully eliminate at least the Pershing IIs from any agreed U.S. deployment of intermediate range missiles, and whether the US can secure the dismantling or destruction of the surplus SS-20s, rather than allowing the Soviets to move them across the Urals into Asia.

Since it has been difficult for Moscow to credibly justify the deployment of the SS-20s on grounds other than that it sought to establish clear theater nuclear superiority in Europe rather than maintaining parity (which has been its rather lame explanation), the deployment of more than 500 US Pershing IIs and cruise missiles that the SS-20 deployment paralleled now threatens to more than nullify the Soviet edge. Hence, the Soviet Union is more likely to enter into an agreement that relinquishes a putative advantage if the alternative (which now clearly seems to be the case) is not only its complete nullification, but also an increased perception of threat. For this reason, some sort of agreement along the lines of the informal Nitze-Kvitsinsky proposals of last year may well constitute the core of an agreement at this level.

One additional point on why the Soviet Union is unlikely to accept radical reductions in its military capabilities. The military prowess of the Soviet Union not only sustains the Soviet role and status in the international system, but it is also the foundation upon which rests the power of the current dominant coalition in the Kremlin. The reduction of Soviet military power will be perceived not only as weakening the prestige of the Soviet Union but also as undermining the power and

status of the Soviet military-industrial complex inside
the Soviet system. At this point both domestic and
external forces intersect and reenforce one another
against deep military cuts.

NOTES

1. G. Arbatov, "The External Expansion of Capital
and Imperialist Policy," Pravda, February 5, 1983.
2. As cited by H. and W. Scott, The Soviet Armed
Forces, (2nd Edition, Praeger, 1981), p. 67.
3. This section of the Constitution, like other
provisions, is full of Soviet ideological code-words
that require explanation:

1) "Consolidating the positions of world socialism,"
is the legal equivalent of what is known as the
"Brezhnev Doctrine," i.e., the right of the Soviet
Union to maintain its hegemony over the lesser
communist states and to intervene to preserve
communist systems wherever they exist.

2) "Supporting the struggle of peoples for national
liberation and social progress," should be
translated to mean the obligation of the Soviet
Union to intervene in the Third World to support
insurrectionary movements ("national liberation") or
support internal attempts to establish communist
rule ("social progress"), i.e. the right to "export
revolution" generally.

3) "Preventing wars of aggression," should be read
to mean the Soviet right or obligation to deter
intervention (military or otherwise) by other powers
on behalf of their client regimes or insurrectionary
movements, i.e., to deter what Moscow calls the
"export of counter-revoulution."

4. Joseph Kraft, "Letter From Moscow," The New
Yorker, January 31, 1983.
5. Cf. V.V. Aspaturian, "The Evolution of Soviet
National Security Decision-Making Under Stalin," in J.
Valenta and W. Potter (editors), Soviet Decision-Making
for National Security (Allen and Unwin, forthcoming,
1983).

5. Eastern Europe at the Crossroads: Contradictory Tendencies of Subservience and Autonomy

Trond Gilberg

Introduction

The relationship between the Soviet Union and the Communist Party of the Soviet Union (CPSU), on the one hand, and the states and ruling parties of Eastern Europe, on the other hand, is becoming increasingly complicated as the decade of the 1980s matures. Western scholarship on the topic reflects this increasing complexity. While in the 1950s and early 1960s most scholars emphasized the voluntary or enforced subservience of the East European states and parties to the Soviet state and the CPSU, and research in the second half of the 1960s and the decade of the seventies stressed nationalism and the quest for autonomy, the focus now is on the fact that subservience exists in certain fields, and a search by the East Europeans for autonomy continues in other areas of the relationship. Add to this the fact that the subservience-autonomy relationships are different for elites, subelites, and the general mass of the population; consider also the fact that each state and party in the region has a set of relations with Moscow that is, at least in part, unique. The resulting complexities are not easily unravelled.[1]

Patterns of Subservience -- Enforced and Voluntary

Much has been written on the elements of subservience in the relationship between Moscow and the capitals of Eastern Europe. The basic parameters of this relationship are known, although we have little concrete evidence about the "gray areas," when East European actions at the state and party levels may produce Soviet intervention or, alternatively, provoke merely sharp commentary, or no response at all from the Kremlin. The clearcut cases, demanding a determined Soviet response, have been outlined by a number of scholars in the West, as follows:

1. Any state leadership which attempts to declare neutrality in foreign policy matters, coupled with moves designed to remove that state from the Comecon and the

Warsaw Pact, will produce a strong Soviet reaction at
the state level, up to and including military
intervention;[2]

2. Any serious challenge to the political hegemony
of the local communist party will be met with resolute
Soviet action, including military intervention, should
the local leadership prove incapable of handling the
matter;[3]

3. The principle of central planning and political
control over the "commanding heights" of the economy
will be upheld, despite the enormous economic costs
which result from such policies;[4]

4. Ideological deviations from the CPSU "model" will
be permitted if such deviations do not include direct
adherence to another "model," such as that advocated by
the Chinese Communist Party (CCP), and provided that
local deviations do not lead to the direct violation of
conditions 1-3, as discussed above;[5]

5. Expanded economic relations with the West,
particularly in the fields of credits and technology
transfers, must not permit the inflow of _political_ ideas
from the West, so that the four principles discussed
above may be maintained.[6]

All of these principles require constant examination
and supervision from the Kremlin, because the assessment
of intolerable deviations must be a judgement call,
since no really clearcut definition has been established
to cover these contingencies. Such a situation
automatically produces numerous gray areas, in which the
leaderships of the Kremlin and those of the local
communist parties in Eastern Europe "pull and haul"
about permissible policies and ideological outlooks. The
relationship between the states and parties of Eastern
Europe, on the one hand, and the Soviet leaders, on the
other hand, is therefore complex, subtle, and at times a
bargaining relationship. Such interaction, by
definition, involves concessions, demands and mutual
accommodation. It is therefore clear that only part of
the relationship can be described as "subservience,"
while other elements smack of East European aggressivism
in political and socio-economic demands made upon the
patron power. It behooves us, therefore, to make a
concerted effort to unravel those elements of this
complex relationship that may be properly described as
subservience, and thereby establish which facets are
Soviet accommodations and concessions.

East European Elite Assessments of Their Relationships with the Soviet Union and the CPSU

The political elites of Eastern Europe are probably
well aware of their relative unpopularity in significant
elements of the population; the extensive surveillance
mechanisms utilized to define the political attitudes of
the masses must be capable of establishing this fact,

and, in any case, social science research in the East
European states themselves has made this quite clear
during the last decade or more.[7] This lack of support is
based on a number of factors: ideological legitimacy is
rapidly waning in societies whose elites have been
unable to "deliver the goods," whether ideological or
material; this lack of material progress (or uneven
progress, coupled with serious deficiencies in the
consumer goods sector and in agriculture) prevents the
formation and maintenance of instrumental legitimacy;
the process of elite recruitment tends to cast up
colorless bureaucrats of the apparatchik or technocratic
variety, thus precluding charismatic legitimacy;
widespread cynicism about ideology and the outward
persecution of the churches in Eastern Europe prohibit
legitimacy based upon sacred sources. In short, most of
the political elites in Eastern Europe rule on the basis
of force (or the threat of the use of force), a
carefully orchestrated political and cultural
nationalism, and the danger that "excesses" in the
political and socio-economic realms by the masses and
their spokesmen will bring into play the various
sanctions of Moscow, including the use of the Red Army.
Subservience to an external hegemon is therefore
functional for domestic reasons for local political
elites whose power would be destroyed or radically
reduced without the direct or indirect presence of the
hegemon. It is a case of the convergence of Soviet and
East European elite interests in the area of political
and socio-economic orthodoxy and many of the practical
policies which follow.[8]
    It is also clear that the political elites of the
East European states and parties share the Soviet
emphasis on loyalty to the Warsaw Pact, the Comecon, and
the basic features of the Kremlin's foreign policy, at
least to a considerable degree. Membership in the two
multilateral organizations mentioned above represents a
guarantee of the existing political and socio-economic
order of each state in the region, and as such it is an
indispensible element of each elite's strategy for
self-preservation and indeed power enhancement; a truly
neutral Poland, for example, would make short shrift of
the current martial law regime. Furthermore, there are
clear economic benefits derived from membership in the
Comecon; the Soviets are providing the East Europeans
with energy and raw materials at a price below that of
the world market, and the USSR represents a huge
customer for qualitatively inferior East European goods
which are unsellable in the West. It has been argued
that, without Soviet control over the basic trends of
East European economic development, the states of the
region would not be in this position at this time,
hence, economic subservience to Moscow is dysfunctional:
this argument strikes me as fatuous, because the Soviets

were involved, and the East European economies have a thirty year history of dependence on the eastern neighbor, which cannot be undone at once, or without serious economic dislocations, perhaps disasters. Political elites cannot afford to discuss the nostalgia of what might have been, nor do they have the time, inclination, or perhaps even expertise to look at the "long run"; they must be concerned with the short- and-intermediate run, and, in this context, the bilateral relationships with the Soviet Union and the multilateral ties in the Comecon are, at least in part, beneficial.[9]

The View of the Societal Elites and the Masses of the Population

While the political and economic subservience of Eastern Europe to the Soviet Union may be beneficial for the political elites of the region in many instances, there are elements of dysfunction in the relationship as well. This dysfunction results from the fact that the East European political elites have interests which are contradictory to those views enunciated by other societal elites; furthermore, in all of the East European systems there is descrepancy (and, at times, open contradiction) between the political elites and significant subsections of the masses. Depending upon the depth of these intra-elite cleavages and the amount of mass alienation from the politics of the political elite, the rulers of Eastern Europe may find their subservience to the Kremlin to be more of a burden than an advantage. A few illustrations of this complicated relationship are in order:

1. The emphasis on ideological orthodoxy, indoctrination, and control of political and other thought, which is an integral part of Eastern Europe's political subservience to Moscow, is resented by important elements of the cultural and technical intelligentsia. Individuals and groups in the social stratus feel constrained by the supervision exercised by party "hacks." They wish to discuss the problems of modern society without the ideological constraints imposed by the party. Their intellectual and emotional inspiration is often the West. Such resentment of Soviet control, direct or indirect, clearly has a detrimental effect upon the work performance of individuals in this stratum, and, furthermore, it produces the yeast for continuing political ferment throughout the region.[10]

The disenchantment of the intelligentsia is nothing new in Eastern Europe. It represents a long-standing condition which precedes the establishment of communist rule in the region. But at this time, the intelligentsia is an indispensible part of the performance of each system, and this key element, therefore, is much more important than it was in the past, so that

disenchantment, apathy, and resentment emanating from
this stratum because of subservience to Moscow now
represent a serious problem in all of the East European
political systems.[11]
   2. The integration of the East European economies
with the Soviet economy reduces the capabilities of
planners and economic managers to deal with local crises
as well as more systemic economic problems, thus
reducing or eliminating the possibility for meaningful
economic performance and the political legitimacy that
attends such performance. Economic reforms, which would
likely have improved productivity, have been abandoned
as a result of Soviet objections. The continued high
East European contributions to the Warsaw Pact clearly
strain the local economies, and, in recent years,
increasing investments in joint ventures in the Comecon
(many of them located on Soviet territory) have reduced
the performance capabilities of the East European
systems at home. And the presence of political
subservience also prevents more fundamental economic
reforms, such as a scaling down of collectivized
agriculture and a corresponding increase in the private
sector, or redirection of investments towards consumer
goods and services. This, in turn, is directly related
to popular perceptions of the political elites
themselves, further reducing the already skimpy fund of
mass support which may still exist.[12]
   3. Political and socio-economic subservience to
Moscow grates on the sensibilities of many individual
leaders themselves, creating severe cross pressures in
their minds and inconsistencies in their actions. As the
systems of the region come of age, so to speak, their
political leaders attempt to anchor themselves in
nationalism, partly because this is functional in terms
of their relationships with the masses, but also because
many of these leaders have spent their political
apprenticeship at home and therefore feel they are
nationalists and not Moscovites. Subservience to Moscow
is both necessary and psychologically dysfunctional at
the same time. The policies which emanate from such
contradictory patterns and relationships are often
erratic and counterproductive,[13] as we shall see in the
case studies presented below.
   4. While the political elites find the enforced
subservience to Moscow functional in many instances, and
elements of the non-political societal elites realize
the need for some restraint in their expressions of
resentment against such a relationship, the masses of
the East European populations are frequently anti-Soviet
or anti-Russian (or both), and there is a pervasive
resentment of both the level of subservience and the
local political elites' acceptance thereof. Add to this
an often uncritical mass admiration of anything Western,
and the local political elites find themselves in a

situation where their relationship with the general population is severely strained as a result of the omnipresence of Soviet influence at the top. Each political elite in Eastern Europe must carefully weigh the benefits of the "Moscow connection" horizontally and in cross-systemic terms against the costs of this relationship vertically, in intra-systemic terms. Since nationalism seems to be on the rise throughout the region, the costs are catching up with the benefits, without any real prosepct of changing the relationship. This contradictory situation has raised the political temperature throughout the entire region and now constitutes one of the most dangerous and intractable elements of the East European crisis.[14]

5. The political and economic subservience to Moscow is increasingly matched by a smaller, but important, dependence upon the West for credits and technology transfer as well as import of consumer products and agricultural commodities. Such dependence is functional up to a point, insofar as it provides goods and services necessary for the short term survival of the socio-economic order; it may even be functional for Moscow (again up to a point) because it relieves the strained Soviet economy of the need to support a number of failures alone. But it is clear that too much dependence on the West constitutes a significant problem for the political elites of Eastern Europe and the Kremlin alike, insofar as it opens the local economies to "capitalist" scrutiny and further demonstrates the lack of economic success associated with the socialist economic mode. This contradictory set of subservience to east and west has once again put Eastern Europe in an exposed position between the major forces confronting each other on the Continent.[15]

The states and communist parties of the area all face these contradictory trends of subservience and attempted autonomy, but in different degrees and with different "mixes" of factors. A detailed analysis of each state and party is required to discover the particularities and peculiarities of these trends.

Contradictory Patterns of Subservience: Case Studies
Since the primary focus of this essay is upon degrees of subservience, it is necessary to exclude two of the states and parties of the region at once, since they have successfully removed themselves from most aspects of reliance on the Soviet Union and the CPSU. Yugoslavia and the League of Communists of Yugoslavia (LCY) and Albania and the Albanian Party of Labor (APL) have fashioned their own policies on the issues of politico-ideological orthodoxy, economic planning and centralization, as well as regime control over the population. In most of these areas, the two sets of

states and parties represent the opposite ends of the spectrum in terms of policy, but they do have one element in common, namely successful defiance of the USSR and the CPSU on all of the issues listed above.

There remain, then, the socialist states and people's democracies of Poland, the German Democratic Republic (GDR), Czechoslovakia, Hungary, Romania and Bulgaria, and the ruling Communist parties of these systems. These units will be the focus of the subsequent analysis.

1. The Case of the Maverick That was "Tamed"

During the 1970s, the Romanian regime under Nicolae Ceausescu was often characterized as the maverick within the Comecon and the Warsaw Pact. The Romanian Communist Party (Partidul Communist Roman -- PCR) attempted to mediate in the Sino-Soviet dispute, thereby gaining greater ideological autonomy for itself in this field. Furthermore, Ceausescu repeatedly criticized elements of Soviet foreign policy, directly or indirectly, during this decade; examples include the Romanian position on the Sino-Vietnam War (where Bucharest remained neutral), the continued conflict in the Middle East, including the Yom Kippur War (after the conclusion of which Romania was the only communist-led state in Eastern Europe to maintain diplomatic relations with Israel); the Vietnamese invasion of Kampuchea (which was indirectly condemned by Ceausescu and his colleagues as a violation of the principle of non-interference in domestic affairs); and, finally, Bucharest's views on the Soviet invasion of Afghanistan (which clearly deplored this drastic action, without directly confronting Moscow on such a sensitive issue). Nicolae Ceausescu also refused to follow the Kremlin's formula for increased armaments expenditures, and the PCR leader further demonstrated the relative autonomy of Romania in foreign policy by mere sporadic participation in Warsaw Pact exercises and refusal to allow joint maneuvers of this organization on Romanian soil.[16]

Bucharest went further in its efforts to demonstrate autonomy during this decade. Trade patterns were partly rerouted, so that the Romanians traded less with Comecon countries and more with the West and some countries of the Third World. During this period, the Ceausescu regime acted with great vigor in Africa, Asia, and Latin America, occasionally billing itself as a "third force" and an alternative model for states caught between the competing superpowers in the latters' quest for power and influence. Ceausescu carried out an exhaustive travel diplomacy to enhance his power and influence and to sell Romanian industrial goods and expertise in return for raw materials and fuels. By the middle of the decade Romania had succeeded in extricating itself from economic dependence upon the Soviet Union to an extent unknown elsewhere in Eastern Europe, in particular in oil and other fuels.[17]

This dramatic manifestation of relative autonomy was functional in domestic politics as well, just as domestic political conditions were partly responsible for the fashioning of such policies in the first place. Ceausescu's emphasis on an independent foreign policy was popular among the ethnic Romanians of the country, who relished the notion of a "greater Romania" finally autonomous of the despised Slavs in general and the Russians in particular. Thus, Ceausescu's foreign policy helped bridge the gap between the political elite and other societal elites as well as substantial elements of the general population. It helped mitigate the problems derived from an overly centralized economy, and autocratic regime based on an irrational cult of the personality, widespread corruption and cynicism, and the apathy of a population which had long lived according to the motto "the party pretends to pay us, and we pretend to work." It was also a functional expression of the curious blend of Marxism and Romanian chauvinism concocted by Nicolae Ceausescu. The fervent manifestations of an autonomous foreign policy helped rekindle the kind of patriotism that had been exhibited in Bucharest immediately after the Soviet-led invasion of Czechoslovakia.[18]

Here, then, was a clear case in which a relative lack of subservience directly contributed to the position of the regime at home, or at least it seemd so to a number of Western analysts, this author included.

We may now profitably reassess the analysis of the functionality of Romanian foreign policy during the 1970s. While Nicolae Ceausescu occasionally carried out policies which were different in degree from those of the Soviet Union, these policies were, at the same time, dysfunctional to Western interests and therefore at least indirectly functional for the Soviet Union and the CPSU. This was certainly the case in Africa, Asia and Latin America, where Bucharest liberally supported a number of liberation movements which were opposed to Western allies. (It may of course be argued that the West should have had the foresight to extend support to these movements as well, thus forestalling the expansion of communism there, but this is a topic which goes far beyond the tasks of this paper.) In the case of the Sino-Soviet dispute, Romanian mediation, if successful, would have brought these two Communist giants together -- hardly an unwelcome prospect for Moscow if it could have allowed the Soviet leaders to reduce the danger on the "eastern front" without any real concessions in ideological terms (which is indeed what Ceausescu argued through his emphasis on the right of each party to define its road to socialism and communism -- a solution which would also have precluded Chinese criticism of Moscow). In any case, a partial settlement of the Sino-Soviet dispute would have ushered in the likelihood of much closer Soviet supervision of various mavericks in Eastern Europe, and on this basis it may be asked if Ceausescu's policies were logical and functional for Romanian interests. In the Sino-Vietnamese conflict, the Romanian position may be defined as simply an attempt to produce order in a chaotic Communist movement, thus reducing the danger of a real conflagration among Communist-led states. It can certainly be argued that such a "cooling of tempers" would be in the Soviet interest as well. Similar interpretations may be offered for Bucharest's policies in the Kampuchean problem. And the Romanian uneasiness with the invasion of Afghanistan had to with the principle of non-interference in domestic affairs, not with the imposition of communist rule -- Bucharest was clearly interested in the latter. The same distinction should be made with reference to Ceausescu's flirtation with "Eurocommunism;" here, he once again emphasized the principle of "national roads," but specifically and vociferously denied that the pluralistic notions of Berlinguer[19] and Carillo had had any validity in Bucharest.

This reevaluation has made it possible to suggest that the relative autonomy of Bucharest was partly functional for the Kremlin -- perhaps as functional as the traditional subservience of pre-1960s Bucharest had been -- and therefore tolerated by Moscow. That such a policy helped enhance the stature of the most orthodox regime in Eastern Europe (Albania excepted) at home was also in the Soviet interest. This is not to deny the real conflicts which did arise in the relationship between Bucharest and Moscow; there are a number of cases in which Soviet commentators were quite blunt and to the point on this score. But it is[20] possible that there is less here than meets the eye.

In any case, the maverick position of the PCR and the Romanian state began to falter after the middle of the 1970s, and by the early 1980s, significant modifications had taken place. The economic policy of greater reliance on the West foundered on the fact that the Romanians had little to sell that really interested the West Europeans or the Americans. Unwise investments and an inefficient economic system reduced the productive capabilities of the Romanian economy and resulted in a dangerous level of dependence upon the West for credits and technology transfer. Bucharest's emphasis on obtaining fuels and raw materals outside the Comecon resulted in fundamental problems after the dramatic rise in oil prices in the 1970s and the fall of the Shah in Iran (who had been one of Romania's principal providers of oil on a barter basis). Increased indebtedness to the West threatened to reduce the capability of Romania to act as a sovereign economic entity. The problems of Poland and the expanding furor of the East European dissident movement loomed large and threatening in repressive Romania, where nepotism and the personality cult were becoming standard features of the regime.[21]

The confluence of these problems produced a redirection in Romanian foreign policy that may have been less dramatic than Bucharest's manifestations of autonomy, but hardly less important in the long run. Ceausescu's protestations of independence became less strident, while his condemnation of imperialism and Western machinations increased in frequency and emphasis. His support for various liberation movements escalated as well. In the Warsaw Pact and the Comecon, the Romanians showed greater willingness to cooperate, and the country's trade was once again focused more on its Communist partners. Negotiations were held with the Soviet Union to obtain oil from that source, in order to reduce Romania's dependence upon the Middle East and other suppliers demanding payment in hard currency. The harsh economic necessities of the 1980s, then, forced the maverick of the previous decade back "in the fold," at least to a degree unknown since the early 1960s. It is a classical case of the political elites accepting a form of foreign policy subservience in return for certain economic benefits.[22]

The readjustments which have taken place in Romanian foreign policy have had varying effects in the non-political societal elites of the country as well as the masses of the population. While most members of the technical and scientific intelligentsia have a Western orientation in general, there has emerged a feeling among many in this group that the maverick foreign policy of Romania has been costly at home, and that such a policy has deprived the country of some economic advantages obtained by more subservient members of the Comecon, notably in the field of energy supplies. These individuals have also noted that economic reform has been possible, even encouraged, elsewhere, with greatly beneficial results, while Romania, under the constraints of its expansive foreign policy, has remained highly centralized, orthodox, and inefficient at home. For the masses, too, the once beguiling notions of "greater Romania" and nationalist chauvinism have worn thin under the constant strain of economic hardship. During my last visit to Romania, a widely circulating joke focused on the need for the country to be "liberated" by the Soviet Union, just like Hungary, so that one could find meat in the stores. Such attitudes do not yet reflect a groundswell of public opinion, and they are unlikely to force significant changes in the Ceausescu regime's

policy on their own, but they do signify the possibility
that, for the first time in a long while, greater
subservience to Moscow (albeit in a limited way) may be
congruent with popular attitudes, provided that it opens
up the path to real economic reform.[23]

2. Subservience and Reform: The Case of Hungary

Hungary represents a striking example of the fact
that foreign policy subservience may be highly
functional at home, provided that it is accompanied by
significant economic reforms. Born of the most clearcut
case of foreign policy deviance yet seen in Eastern
Europe, the Kadar regime quickly established its
credentials in the Kremlin, and Budapest has been a
loyal, if moderate, supporter of Soviet foreign policy
ever since, both at the state and interparty levels.
This kind of loyalty has made it possible for the
Hungarian leadership to exercise considerable moderation
domestically, which has manifested itself as a
successful economic reform, with a considerable amount
of decentralization, a renewed emphasis on agriculture,
and an investment and remuneration policy that has made
economic efforts in crucial economic sectors worthwhile
for the individual producer. The cultural policy of the
Kadar regime has made considerable pluralism possible,
and even the party itself has experienced
diversification of opinion without serious disagreements
on fundamentals. The result has been a relative success
story up to the present. While Hungary has not exhibited
the political dynamism of Poland up to December 1981, it
has avoided the crisis now engulfing that Baltic
country, and the dead-end economic catastrophe of the
Polish system can be contrasted with relatively
prosperous Hungary (which has its problems, notably of
foreign indebtedness, but no fundamental crisis, as
yet).[24]

The policies of the political elite, which combine
relative external subservience with domestic reform have
fairly broad support among societal elites and the
masses of the population. The technical and managerial
intelligentsia are Western oriented in general terms,
and may therefore resent Hungarian subservience to the
Soviet Union in principle, but the possibilities for
domestic economic and managerial reform made possible,
at least in part, by this subservience enables these
elites to practice "Western" theories of production and
management, and this is clearly more important than
symbolic foreign policy autonomy. Similarly, the
anti-Soviet attitudes of most of the population at large
are well known, but they exist at the theoretical, not
the practical, level; submission to the Kremlin in the
foreign policy arena allows the Hungarian worker to eat
goulash while joking about the despised Ivans. Here,

then, foreign policy subservience has been functional for political and socio-economic elites as well as the general population.[25]

3. The Necessity of Subservience: The Case of the GDR
While foreign policy subservience is functional for the economic well-being of Hungary (and hence for the relative legitimacy of the Kadar regime), such a relationship is indispensable in the case of the GDR. As has often been pointed out, the GDR has struggled against the fact that it is an artificial creation whose political order would not have existed without the protection of the Soviet Union. The substantial Soviet troop deployments in the GDR remain a forceful indicator of this crucial fact. At the same time, the East German regime struggles mightily to ensure its own existence through tight ideological control and massive political socialization, in an effort to establish and nurture a separate East German political culture and conscience. The sealing of the GDR's borders over twenty years ago was designed to stop the hemorrhage of the most productive population elements to the West, but it was also an effort to bring home the message to the population: the GDR is here to stay, so you must turn your energies to the domestic sector, thereby improving your lot here at home, since you cannot go there, to the West. Since that time the East Germans have experienced relative economic prosperity, and the regime has produced a number of managerial experiments which helped ensure productivity while maintaining the centralized nature of both the economic and political systems.[26]

While the political elites of the GDR thus depended upon their subservience to the Soviet Union and the CPSU in state policy and interparty affairs, the technical and managerial intelligentsia likewise supported a system that provided them with a certain amount of autonomy in their decision making, accorded them a number of economic privileges and rapid promotions, and elevated the GDR to a position of economic leadership in the Eastern bloc. The problems of subservience, therefore, did not primarily arise in inter-elite relations in the domestic system, but rather in the attitudes and values of the general population, which was traditionally anti-Russian and now anti-Soviet, confused about its real political entity (due to its continued close relationship with the "other" (Germans), and resentful of the political elite's close ties with the Soviets. It was in this relationship that the Honecker leadership faced its stiffest test, and it was here that meaningful policies had to be fashioned. Such policies have in fact been attempted during the 1970s and 1980s, the main manifestations of which can be summarized as follows:

a. Emphasis on the relationship between the "progressive" elements of the German historical tradition of the GDR. In this sense, the "new socialist state on German soil" is billed as the final fruition of traditional German progressivism, presumably an appeal to those elements of the East German population that are not Communist but also not unalterably opposed to the present order. As one observer in East Berlin once remarked: "We got not only Rosa Luxembourg, Karl Liebknecht, Karl Marx and Friedrich Engels, but also Mozart, Brahms, and the great thinkers. The West Germans got Hitler and the Kaiser."[27]

b. A conscious build-up of East German pride in the achievements of the regime in educational and economic terms, especially in comparison with the other socialist systems. Pankow has been known to lecture the other East Europeans on proper economic management, ideological correctness, and propriety; during the Polish crisis in 1980-81, the veiled criticism produced by the regime against the vacillations of the Warsaw leadership was matched by less polite references in the general public to those "Polacks" who don't want to work. These were clearly resurrections of age-old animosities, but may have been manifestations of pride in the achievements of this era as well.[28]

c. East Berlin bills itself as the junior partner of the Soviets in the Warsaw Pact, the Comecon, and in political leadership and activity elsewhere. This kind of appeal may not carry much weight in the general population with its traditional anti-Soviet attitudes, but may be of considerable value in recruiting those opportunistic and upwardly mobile elements who have accepted the geopolitical "givens" of the GDR and now hope to make the best out of the existing situation. These are likely to be the ambitious individuals needed by the regime, and thus may help the latter's leaders bridge the gap between elite and mass.[29]

d. Connected to (c.) above is the emphasis put on East German activities in many areas of the Third World, particularly sub-Saharan Africa, but also the Middle East and Central America. This activity, which emphasizes the East German role in establishing medical facilities and training administrative cadres in countries of need, is a resurrection of the old German tradition of "enlightened colonialism" under the auspices of "progressive fraternal aid." This policy emphasizes facets rather different from the Soviet involvement in the same areas and therefore helps put the GDR on the map independently of the eastern superpower. It is likely that such policies, with their attendant

publicity, will have some effect in instilling pride
and national consciousness in the general
population, and it clearly helps counter-balance the
image of complete East German subservience to the
Soviet Union.[30]

It is unclear how successful the regime has been in
reversing or modifying the widely held belief that the
GDR is overly subservient in relations with the Soviet
Union, but the combination of a high level of
modernization, a superbly educated population, a
tradition of duty and subservience to authority, and
feelings of superiority vis-à-vis eastern neighbors (now
seemingly demonstrated in economic performance) have
combined to produce relative stability in the GDR, as
contrasted with the open turmoil of Poland and the
gathering crisis elsewhere in the region.

4. Subservience and the Survival of Regimes: The Case of
Poland.
In all three cases examined so far, there is a
dynamic interaction between domestic and foreign policy
consideration, in which the political elites of each
country find external or domestic subservience to the
Soviet "model" to be functional in some degree. But
Poland was and is different. There, very few individuals
find dependence on the Soviet Union and the CPSU
acceptable; the political elites of Poland have always
striven for greater autonomy from the Soviets,
especially in domestic politics, and many of the
societal elites of Poland also find this relationship
with the Eastern neighbor distasteful. The anti-Russian
and anti-Soviet attitudes of the general population are
well known and need no further elaboration here. In
other words, there was in Poland a relative congruence
of the attitudes of elites and masses alike on the
question of subservience to the Soviet Union and the
CPSU.
This congruence of attitudes had a number of effects
which ultimately brought the political and socio-
economic order of Poland to the brink of disaster. The
geopolitical realities of the country, coupled with the
demonstrated willingness and capability of the Soviet
Union to maintain the status quo of the region,
presented the Polish political leadership with Moscow,
especially since Poland is the linchpin of the Kremlin's
military organization in Eastern Europe as well as an
indispensable communications link with the Soviet troops
in the GDR. But this enforced subservience further
alienated a population (and most societal elites) which
had already reached the limits of its tolerance of
economic mismanagement and unending problems in the
agricultural sector and the provision of consumer goods.
The result was a half decade in which the disenchanted

population and an activated working class made a real
alliance with the politically mobilized intelligentsia,
forcing the party leadership into retreat on a number of
policy questions, especially in the economic realm,
which ultimately ended in the disaster of martial law.[31]
The result of December 1981 was a major anomaly. The
Polish political elite ceased to function as such, and
was shunted aside by military authorities -- a first in
European communist systems. Furthermore, the Jaruzelski
leadership became fundamentally dependent upon the
Soviet Union while deeply resenting this fact. This
subservience to the Kremlin was not based upon
accomodation for mutual benefit, as is the case in
Hungary, nor upon ideological affinity with the
Stalinist model, which is the case in Romania, but, in
the Polish case, it is merely a question of the survival
of a _Polish_ regime, _any_ Polish regime, in the face of
threatened Soviet interventions. Here, then, is a case
of foreign policy subservience designed to preserve the
vestiges of national existence -- indeed a unique
situation in the region of Eastern Europe.[32]

5. Subservience and the Errant Pupil: The Case of Czechoslovakia

Only two states in Eastern Europe have been invaded
by Soviet and Warsaw Pact troops since the establishment
of Communist power in the region, and both of these have
experienced subsequent scrutiny by the Kremlin to an
extent which necessitated subservience in foreign
policy, both at the state and interparty levels. But,
once again, Hungary is the only state in the region
whose leaders have been capable of maximizing this kind
of foreign policy relationship at home, through the
institution of a relatively successful economic reform.
Czechoslovakia, on the other hand, has refrained from
any major experiments in the econmic realm while
reestablishing political control at home and emphasizing
ideological orthodoxy in the relations between the
political elite and the rest of society. The current
political culture of Czechoslovakia is characterized by
high levels of apathy among the masses of the population
and many members of societal elites, such as the
technical, managerial, and cultural intelligentsia, and
a few real attempts at meaningful opposition (most of
which was dealt with rather severly during the 1970s).
More than usual, then, the political elites of
Czechoslovakia function in a political vacuum, separated
from the general population and most of the non-
political societal elites by a massive chasm.[33]
The isolation of the political elite makes foreign
policy subservience to the Soviet Union and the CPSU
both functional and necessary. There can be no doubt
that the current leadership in Prague has little support
in the masses of the population, and its continued

survival at the top is dependent upon the political
facts of life, which involve the special relationship
with Moscow. By the same token, this very relationship
appears dysfunctional for most societal elites and also
the general population, whose anti-Sovietism, albeit of
rather recent vintage, is firmly imbedded, formed as it
was in the crucible of armed intervention. The resulting
discrepancies between the interests of the political
elite and those of the rest of society represent sources
of instability and potential for serious political
trouble.

All political elites faced with this kind of a
problem attempt to devise policies which can deal with
it. In Hungary, resentment generated from foreign policy
subservience to the Soviet Union and the CPSU is
mitigated through domestic reform and relative economic
success; in Romania, relative foreign policy autonomy
and nationalism have helped alleviate dissatisfaction
emanating from tight ideological control and an abysmal
economic performance; in the GDR, subservience abroad is
alleviated by domestic economic performance and the role
of the republic as the junior partner of Moscow in the
Third World and a model for others in the Comecon and
the Warsaw Pact. The Polish military regime has no
solution except the specter of extinction of the nation
as a politcal unit. The Czechoslovak elite's policy
seems to focus on depoliticization as a strategy for
dealing with the problems arising out of foreign policy
subservience to a despised hegemon. Widespread political
apathy is tolerated as long as economic performance does
not suffer unduly, and the regime appears more devoted
to a strategy of "muddling through" than of development
and rule. There has also been a conscious effort to
increase the availability of consumer goods,
particularly foodstuffs, as a palliative to politically
dissatisfied individuals and groups. Thus, nobody works
with a great deal of enthusiasm, but most people work
part of the time, and there is no immediate threat of a
political and economic conflagration. The relatively
quiescent nature of the Czech political culture (and
also in part of the Slovak culture) makes eruptions less
likely than in volatile Poland. On the other hand, the
reliance on importation of foodstuffs and consumer
goods, without the necessary upgrading of the
Czechoslovak export industries, bodes ill for the future
and throws into question the strategy of producing
political quietude through borrowed consumption.
Czechoslovakia may indeed become a real economic problem
in the intermediate run, say in a decade. Then, the
foreign policy dependence of this state on the Soviet
Union will become costly, both for Prague and for
Moscow.[34]

6. Accepted Subservience: The Case of Bulgaria

Bulgarian relations with the Soviet Union and the CPSU remain close in the 1980s, and this closeness appears to reflect adjustment to the facts of geopolitics and ideology, both on the part of the politcal and societal elites and the masses of the population. Analysts have pointed out the traditional pro-Russianism of the Bulgarian masses as one of the major reasons for this close relationship. Furthermore, the economic ties which have developed between Sofia and Moscow are now so many and so close that the Bulgarian economy could not possibly survive without them. In fact, one may speak of partial economic integration of the two economies, with close cooperation also between the planning agencies in both countries.[35]

These ties have brought considerable economic benefit to Bulgaria, through the transfer of Soviet technology, equipment, and know-how; there is, furthermore, economic aid, the provision of most of Bulgaria's energy needs (at relatively low rates of pay), and a Soviet market which can always be counted upon to accept export goods from the Balkan neighbor. The result has been a rather rapid rise in the Bulgarian standard of living, so that by now, Bulgaria has surpassed Romania in certain measures of this standard, such as available foodstuffs and some consumer goods.[36]

The Bulgarians have reciprocated by unusually high levels of ideological and political support for Moscow in all major areas of concern and all major political issues of the 1970s and 1980s. The Bulgarian regime, then, is the staunchest supporter of the Soviet Union and the CPSU in all of Eastern Europe.[37] This foreign policy subservience has been functional in economic terms and, since there is relatively little anti-Russianism in the general population, it has not created the kinds of political dysfunction which similar dependence produced in Poland and some other states of the region. But despite these advantages of subservience, the relationship with Moscow may yet turn out to be dysfunctional in the long run. It is to this problem that the discussion now turns.

Eastern Europe at the Crossroads: The Necessity and Dysfunctionality of Foreign Policy Subservience to the the Soviet Union and the CPSU

The scope of the problem

As discussed above, foreign policy dependence upon Moscow is a necessity in Eastern Europe in the 1980s, enforced by Soviet determination to protect its empire and needed by political elites whose unpopularity at home demands a protector, a hegemon which can eliminate any alternatives to these elites' continued rule. Even the economies of the region desperately need the Soviet

Union; only the Soviet economy is big enough to supply
the raw materials, fuels, and emergency credits needed
in the region during this decade while at the same time
ensuring the continuation of the socio-economic and
political order of Eastern Europe. The West, burned by
overextended credit to the region during the 1970s, is
unlikely to extend further massive credits (except to
help ensure the repayment of existing debts), and, in
any case, such credit will now only be provided if
greater control and information about the internal
operation of each economic system are forthcoming -- a
rather unlikely scenario in the secretive world of
planned economies. There remains the Soviet Union, which
is in a better position to provide such economic aid,
because of the congruence of its political and
socio-economic systems with those of Eastern Europe. The
major question is Soviet capability.

The problem of capabilities arises because of the
enormity of the problem. It is no exaggeration to state
that the political and economic systems of Eastern
Europe are in fundamental crisis unlike other problems
which have existed in the region previously. While rapid
economic expansion was possible in earlier decades
primarily through extensive development (the building of
new if inefficient factories staffed by the swelling
ranks of labor newly recruited from the countryside),
such expansion can now only come from intensive
development (higher productivity from each worker).
Demographic developments in almost all of the East
European states demand such a shift, but the weakness of
the agricultural sector and the insufficiency of the
consumer goods and service industries of the region
reduce the likelihood of the shift being successful,
since incentives (in the form of foodstuffs or better
consumer goods) are largely lacking. Other areas of
possible reform, which might enhance the performance of
the economy, include decentralization in planning and
implementation and a greater reliance on a modified
market, significant changes in investment priorities,
with greater emphasis on agriculture and the service
sector, and an attempt to stem the flow of manpower from
the countryside to the cities, with a further emphasis
on retaining young and qualified individuals on the
land.

Economic shortcomings are closely related to
political problems, which in turn stem from low
legitimacy, resentment of foreign policy dependence on
the Soviet Union, widespread corruption and cynicism,
and the emerging "amoral familism" of individuals who
feel that the regime is exploiting them, and thus
deserves no services in return, while the close family
and friends must be protected against the exploitative
political order. Meaningful political reform would
therefore need to include greater opportunities for real

participation by groups and individuals now outside the
mainstream of the political order, greater regime
willingness to allow divergent (if still system-
supportive) views to be heard, and improved administrative services and less repressive methods of dealing
with those who somehow stand outside of the established
political framework. Finally, there is a need for
greater foreign policy autonomy, without a direct
challenge to Soviet hegemony in the region.

The need for reform outlined above vastly exceeds
the capabilities of the current socio-economic and
political order to accommodate it short of fundamental
transformation of the systems of the region. Put
differently, the needed reforms are structurally
interrelated and should be implemented as a package, but
the package cannot be accommodated within the existing
structures and procedures of the Communist-led systems
in Eastern Europe. Since both the Kremlin and the local
political leaders have postulated the continuation of
the present political arrangements in the region, only
some reforms may be instituted, or, conversely, minor
"tinkering" with all of the possibilities discussed
above will be allowed. In either case, it is likely that
the efforts produced will be insufficient for the
challenges posed. The result will be more "muddling
through," which cannot come to grips with the problems
at hand. The analyst, therefore, must ask how long such
makeshift policies can continue to hold the line against
the systemic tide of difficulties. The foreign policy
relations with the Soviet Union and the CPSU are
directly related to this fundamental question.

Policy Options and their Prospects

Since the basic nature of the political and
socio-economic systems in Eastern Europe is
predetermined to a considerable degree, policy options
available to deal with the current and future crises in
the region are limited. Some of the options available
within these confines are:

a. Cautious experimentation with decentralization of
   economic management. This kind of experimentation
   will be limited to elements which do not alter
   fundamental political realities, such as continued
   political control over economic management, and
   predominance of the center over other economic
   units.

b. Fairly significant investment programs in fields
   such as agriculture. These programs will have only
   limited impact unless other factors, such as a
   redirection of the population flow back to the
   countryside, can also be accomplished (I here refer
   primarily to the need for more highly qualified,
   relatively young individuals to move back into the
   village.

c. Various schemes for increased productivity may be tried, including more varied remuneration systems and a number of symbolic ways of providing individual and group recognition. Such schemes will also have a more limited effect if meaningful economic incentives are not forthcoming.

d. Increased efforts of integration and product specialization in the Comecon, so that existing expertise can be better utilized. Such efforts will likely run afoul of the growing tide of nationalism in the region.

e. Continuing efforts to improve the quality of production of finished goods, so that they may become competitive in Western markets. There is a substantial literature discussing why such efforts are unlikely to succeed.

f. Attempts to obtain additional Western technology and credit, so that better productivity can be achieved in the framework of the existing order. I have already mentioned some reasons why this option is becoming more limited as the current crisis lingers on.[38]

In the political realm, limited efforts of expanded participation for groups and individuals are most likely to take the form of cooptation into the party, and actual political competition and choice in a limited way at the local level, with little or no opportunity for such competition elsewhere. Furthermore, greater willingness to allow relative autonomy for individuals and groups inside the existing system will not signify the possibility of elites granting opportunities for real change.[39]

These options are limited precisely because of East European subservience to the Soviet Union and the CPSU in the foreign policy arena. By contrast, the problems of lack of legitimacy, lagging productivity, cynicism, corruption, overcentralization and mismanagement are fundamental ones which require nothing less than drastic changes in the existing political and socio-economic order. It therefore seems clear that the options available to East European policy makers in the 1980s will be inadequate to solve the massive problems of the region. What, then, will be the nature of politics in the area during the remainder of this decade?

Eastern Europe in the 1980s: Pushing Back the Crossroads Choices

Confronted by problems that demand fundamental changes in policy, but prevented from producing such policies by their foreign policy subservience to the Soviet Union and the CPSU, the political elites of Eastern Europe find themselves in an unenviable situation resembling the infamous "catch-22." The piecemeal reforms which may be introduced can help offset some of the less fundamental problems of this decade, but cannot come to grips with the fact that the current systemic crisis involves multiple subcrises, each appearing beyond solution at the moment; there is the crisis of legitimacy, followed by the crisis of commitment, and matched by the economic crisis of productivity and consumption. These problems will most likely send the states and parties of the region caroming from problem to problem, with policies that vacillate between conciliation and repression, reform and retrenchment. Throughout all of this, the leaders in the Kremlin will be watching uneasily, attempting to establish credible policies in their front yard. These leaders may appear vacillating and unsure of their approaches, and this would be understandable, for their empire is indeed in the throes of extremely difficult times. Western leaders and scholars would do well to remember, nevertheless, that vacillation is not the same as weakness, and that the Kremlin is prepared to act with the requisite firmness to prevent the problems of the region from undermining its hold on the area. The following are a few major points which will most likely guide Soviet actions in the region during the remainder of this decade:

1. Eastern Europe is an area of primary concern to the Soviet Union, but a secondary priority for the United States and Western Europe. The Soviets will therefore take all the necessary steps, no matter how costly in terms of military, economic and prestige expenditures, to ensure the continuation of the status quo. Since the area is secondary to the West, we will not take the risks involved in utilizing the present crisis in the region to our advantage (if advantage is defined as increased East European autonomy). The foregin policy subservience of the states and parties of the region will continue.

2. The current level of foreign policy autonomy in Eastern Europe is considered tolerable by the Soviet leadership, now that the immediate Polish crisis has been "solved." We can therefore expect that such diversity as now exists in this field will be permitted to continue, perhaps even expand somewhat. But there are definite limits. No state in the region will be allowed to slip out of the Soviet sphere, as defined in the beginning of this discussion. The political elites of the region realize the definite Soviet commitment to holding the line here, and they will do their utmost to observe, since their own survival and that of their regimes depend on such acquiescence.

3. Unsolvable problems may be postponed for a long time. While it is true that the problems facing the regimes of Eastern Europe today can only be solved through far-ranging changes in the existing political

and socio-economic order, the solution can be postponed for a number of years, perhaps even decades, as long as the political elites retain control over the means of coercion and exhibit firm willingness to use them. Lack of legitimacy does not imply lack of control; unarmed, disgruntled workers can only win over armed, disciplined soldiers in the long run. Thus, to paraphrase a well-known saying: the situation in Eastern Europe is critical, but not serious. Those who hope to see "the window of vulnerability" close by itself because of internal difficulties in the Soviet bloc during this decade should prepare themselves for a longer wait or other methods of window closing.

4. The very nature of the problems confronting the poltical elites of Eastern Europe in the 1980s will force greater cohesion on the bloc, not less. This condition will nevertheless be temporary; at some point beyond this decade, centrifugal forces such as nationalism and the quest for national roads to socialism and communism will become much stronger, and may force a reassessment of bilateral and multilateral relationships in the region.

5. Since the fissions of the bloc will become serious only several years (or more) from now, the leadership in the Kremlin, rejuvenated by the post-Andropov generation, has the opportunity to design preventative policies in Eastern Europe itself, or, alternatively, to fashion its relationship with the West in such a way that the challenges (real or perceived) that emanate from that quarter may be blunted. One way to accomplish such a goal would be to weaken the Western alliance itself. Recent Soviet foreign policy approaches towards the West, and particularly towards Western Europe, have shown that the Kremlin will not stand idly by while the crisis of the eastern systems in Europe moves inexorably towards its conclusion. Nothing helps alleviate problems at home more effectively than foreign policy successes. The Soviet Union, behind its shield of burgeoning military power, and faced by a Western alliance which continues to experience considerable problems in its efforts to produce common policies, is in a position to produce such successes in a number of areas of the world. If it does, it can also be expected to tighten the ropes in its own alliance. The elites and peoples of Eastern Europe live with the practical knowedge of this possibility every day.

99

NOTES

1. An example of this kind of analysis is Vernon V. Aspaturian, "Has Eastern Europe Become a Liability to the Soviet Union: The Political-Ideological Aspects," in Charles Gati (ed.), The International Politics of Eastern Europe (New York, N.Y.: Praeger Publishers, 1976), pp. 17-37.
2. I have discussed this in "The Political Order" in Stephen Fischer-Galati (ed.), Eastern Europe in the 1980s Boulder, Colo.: Westview Press, 1981), pp. 121-124.
3. Ibid.
4. Ibid.
5. See ibid. and also an excellent analysis by Heinz Timmermann, "Proletarischer Internationalismus aus Sowjetischer Sicht: Eine Historisch-Politische Analyse," Berichte des Bundesinstituts für Ostwissenschaftliche und Internationale Fragen, No, 3-1983.
6. An interesting discussion of the principles of such transfer can be found in Philip Hanson, "Technology Transfer to the Soviet Union," in Survey, Vol. 23, No. 2 (Spring 1977-78), pp. 73-105.
7. At times, cynicism and politcal apathy turn to "social pathology"; see, for example, Piotr Kryczka, "Some Phenomena of Social Pathology in Poland," The Polish Sociological Bulletin, No. 2, 1978, pp. 101-107.
8. This relationship was first discussed by Zbigniew K. Brzezinski in The Soviet Bloc (Cambridge, Mass.: Harvard University Press, 1969), esp. ch. 17, (pp. 433-456).
9. Ibid.
10. Nowhere was this more clear than in Poland. See, for example, Stefan Kisielewski, "Planning under Socialism," in Survey, Vol. 25, No. 1 (Winter 1980), pp. 19-38.
11. E.g., Walter Connor, "Dissent in Eastern Europe: A New Coalition?" Problems of Communism, Jan.-Febr. 1980, pp. 1-18.
12. Ibid.
13. This is clearly the case in Romania; see, for example, my analysis in "The Communist Party of Romania," in Stephen Fischer-Galati (ed.), The Communist Parties of Eastern Europe (New York, N.Y.: Columbia University Press, 1979), pp. 281-327.
14. See Ernst Kux, "Growing Tensions in Eastern Europe," Problems of Communism, Mar.-Apr. 1980, pp. 21-38.
15. The level of this indebtedness has now risen to astronomical proportions; see The New York Times, June 19, 1983.

100

16. These statements represent a summary of many sources; one of the most important of these is Nicolae Ceausescu's speech to the twelfth PCR congress in November, 1979; see Scinteia (Bucharest), Nov. 20, 1979.

17. See my discussion in "The Communist Party of Romania," in Fischer-Galati (ed.), The Communist Parties of Eastern Europe, pp. 281-327.

18. The appeal to this kind of patriotism was clear in Ceausescu's speech to the twelfth congress (see Scinteia, Nov. 20, 1979).

19. One of the most clearcut statements of Ceausescu's views on Eurocommunism can be found in his speech to PCR and state activists, printed in ibid., Aug. 4, 1978.

20. Bucharest's reevaluations have become clear on several issues; an example of this is Ceausescu's indirect acceptance of the Soviet argument in Moscow's controversy with the Italian Communist Party (e.g., Ceausescu's speech, printed in ibid., Jan. 27, 1982).

21. Romanian commentary on Poland has been critical of the pluralism manifested in Polish society, while accepting the principle that each state must decide on its own problems without outside interference. See, for example, an editorial in Scinteia, Dec. 26, 1981, discussing the imposition of martial law in Poland.

22. An oil deal between the Soviet Union and Romania was made public by Moscow in June 1980 and discussed by Cam Hudson in "Soviets Confirm Oil Deal with Romania," Radio Free Europe Research, RAD Background Report/135, (Eastern Europe), June 1980.

23. I cannot reveal the identity of the individuals mentioned at this time.

24. Hungary's successes in agriculture, for example, have made the country an important exporter of wheat to the Soviet Union and other countries in Eastern Europe. The successes here for 1981-82 were discussed in Nepszabadsag, Aug. 18, 1982.

25. An example of Hungarian acceptance of Soviet views on foreign policy matters is Budapest's attitudes attitudes towards Solidarity and political pluralism in Poland, e.g., ibid., April 18, 1981.

26. E.g., Neues Deutschland, (East Berlin), Jan. 16-17, 1982, reporting on the plan fulfillment for the year 1981; see also the journal Einheit (East Berlin) (No. 1, 1982) which discussed in detail the recipe for socialist organization, as seen in Pankow.

27. I have discussed in my chapter, "The Political Order," in Fischer-Galati (ed.), Eastern Europe in the 1980s, pp. 149-156.

28. East German commentary on the Polish "events" has always been ascerbic, e.g., Neues Deutschland, Sept. 8, 1981, discussing Solidarity's congress and the many "anti-state" elements which participated in it.

29. For an interesting discussion of the GDR's roles in foreign affairs, see Woodrow J. Kuhns, "The German Democratic Republic in Africa," (seminar paper, Pennsylvania State University), to be published in East European Quarterly, Winter 1984 (esp. pp. 20-29).

30. Ibid.

31. E.g., Adam Bromke, "Policy and Politics in Gierek's Poland," in Maurice D. Simon and Roger E. Kanet (eds.), Background to Crisis: Policy and Politics in Gierek's Poland (Boulder, Colo.: Westview Press, 1981), pp. 3-27.

32. The Jaruzelski speech which established martial law made this point rather forcefully, and an editorial in Trybuna Ludu (Warsaw) Dec. 14, 1981, emphasized this also.

33. Even Alois Indra, a member of the Presidium of the Czechoslovak Party, admitted this in a recent article in Nove Slovo (Bratislava), No. 10, March 11, 1982).

34. In the fall of 1982, the main Party organ, Rude Pravo (Prague) ran two editorials which admitted serious economic problems (Sept. 10, 1982 and Sept. 13, 1982).

35. The draft theses for the twelfth congress of the Bulgarian Communist Party, published in Rabotnichesko Delo (Sofia), Feb. 16, 1981, made it clear that this close cooperation will continue.

36. I have based this on comparative reviews of a number of indices found in the statistical yearbooks of both countries; a detailed discussion of this topic would go beyond the scope of the present paper.

37. E.g., Bulgarian commentary on Polish events, which matched Soviet statements very closely; e.g., Rabotnichesko Delo, May 31, 1981.

38. An excellent discussion of the problem of technology transfer is Josef C. Brada, "Technologietransfer Zwischen West und Ost," Osteuropa, May 1981, pp. 408-426.

39. E.g., Heinz Timmermann, "Aktuelle Tendenzen im Kommunistischen Parteiensystem: Zerfallsprozesse und Neuorientierungen," Berichte des Bundesinstituts fur Ostwissenschaftliche und Internationale Studien, No. 7-1983.

6. Do Systemic Variables Make a Difference? Causes of Successes and Failures of the East European Communist States

Ivan Volgyes

The purpose of this chapter is to discuss the changing relationship between the superpowers and Europe. My major thesis is to suggest that Eastern Europe has entered a new era in which the national decision-making elites in the region must make deliberate choices concerning the future of their countries, their political and economic developments in light of the new realities that govern both superpowers relations with each other and govern the relations of Europe -- both East and West -- with the superpowers.

In this paper, first, I will discuss the various "eras" of economic and social development in Eastern Europe, second, the determinants of the successes and failures of Eastern European policies, highlighting the economic and social changes from the perspectives of theoretical and practical concerns. The major discussion in the third section of the paper will deal with the problem of choice for Eastern Europe, evaluating their opportunities for greater or lesser integration with the West as well as the dangers of choosing either autarchy or integration. In the concluding, last section of the paper an attempt will be made to suggest some guidelines for the West, as to what policies it should follow in order to encourage the development of Eastern Europe that will be in our view most beneficial for the people of the region, as well as, for the future of East-West relations.

Part I. Eras of Social and Economic Change in Eastern Europe

Eastern European political and economic development can be characterized as having passed through four distinct phases. The first era lasted from the beginning of Soviet control to about 1955-1956: this period can best be labeled as the era of Stalinist development. The second period between 1956 and around 1968 saw the reexamination of the Stalinist model and the development of a "native" model, although both successful and failed "deviations" must be noted during this period. The third period lasted approximately until 1980-1982; this era saw relatively rapid changes within the various Eastern European states as they tried to grapple with the "boom" decade of the international economic cycle while preserving power in the hands of the party elite. Finally, the fourth era, begun between 1980-1982, has grappled with the reality of economic decline and pushed the resulting political turmoil in the forefront of decision making for Communist policy-makers of the region.

A. The literature on the Stalinist phase of development, of course, is ample and adequate. The gist of this phase has naturally been the blind following of the Soviet model -- whether imposed or willingly adopted -- in every aspect of socio-economic and political existence. The nationalization of the industries, the banks, the collectivization of land, the urbanization and industrialization attempts intended for the modernization of the countries, the mobilization of society, the establishment of a "loyal" apparatus of power, the development of the totality of planning apparats to attempt to control everything in society, are all well known. What is perhaps not emphasized as frequently is that this phase witnessed the separation of Eastern Europe from the West to a degree unprecedented since the Turkish occupation of the region. Specifically for those countries that have always been thought of as a part of Western European culture (Poland, Czechoslovakia, East Germany, Hungary, parts of Romania, and -- until its break with the Comintern -- even Yugoslavia) were forced to renounce their Western heritage in culture and civilization. The supremacy of the state over society, of society over the individual, and the control of the state over every individual -- concepts completely opposed to Western oriented development but expected of the Eastern model of social existence -- were imposed upon these countries with speed and thoroughness. Added to these societal demands, of course, was the Soviet demand for total autarchy, the physical separation of the region from Western Europe, from Western values, from Western thought and economic-societal models, through the establishment of a real Iron Curtain: the stark reality of minefields, barbed wires and ever-present guard dogs, reemphasizing the total separation, not merely by keeping PEOPLE inside their boundaries but by keeping Western ideas and contacts out of the region.

B. Stalin's death and the "dysfunctions" -- as the Soviet-Communist elite liked to label the tremendous social and political upheavals of the 1950s -- brought about various sets of fundamental questioning into the lives of these regimes. It is important to note that the "events" in Poland and Hungary, just as much as the earlier riots in Czechoslovakia and East Germany and the terrific impact of Khrushchev's de-Stalinization attempts, brought into question the fundamental assumptions of the Communist regimes. If, indeed, as Khrushchev himself said the Soviet model was "fallible," then its blind following certainly was fallible at best, self-destructive and criminal at worst. If the Soviet plans for development and modernization, the intro- duction of total socio-political control and the organization of social existence, or the treatment of nationalities, were fraught with potential pitfalls, then the elites in these states had to reexamine their own targets, strategies and tactics in light of the potential failures that could result from the blind application of Soviet diktats. Whether that process of realization, the recognition of the failures of duplicating the Soviet model, came as a result of revolutionary upheaval -- as in Poland and Hungary -- or as a cautious inter-party examination of the problems of rule -- as it did in the rest of these states -- is immaterial. What is important is that in 1956-1957, in every Communist state there was a debate over the "right" or "correct" method of ruling over these unwitting people.

I emphasize here, "unwitting" for a specific reason, namely my profound conviction that none of the Stalinist or post-Stalinist regimes -- naturally with the exclusion of Imre Nagy's and perhaps Wladyslaw Gomulka's 1956 or Dubcek's 1968 regimes -- ever attained any sense of legitimacy at all. Unlike during the heady days of the immediate post 1945 years, where in some states, at some juncture in their political life, and among at least some segments of the population, the Communists were at last able to garner a sense of grudging acquiescence for their own plans to remold society, in the post-1956 period there was only apathy, distrust and hatred expressed toward these regimes. The albatross of failed models of social development is a heavy burden that no regime can cast off easily. To use an absurd example, the Republican party in the US, following 1932, for several decades was unable to cast off the "blame" for the Great Depression; imagine the views of the Eastern Europeans for the abundant failures clearly visible in their states, for the hunger and scarcity they experienced in their everyday lives and the terror that was ever present and noticeable around them. That they blamed the "Communists" and "communism" for all these failures is also abundantly clear: in Communist states where the party is the "ordinator" or "leading force" of all aspects of social life, there is simply no one else to blame for the ills of socio-political and economic development.

It is, thus, normal to suggest that the forces compelling reexamination of the Soviet model were ascendant during these years; prompted by the

Khrushchevian concessions regarding the applicability of the "different roads to socialism" concept, there were some lively discussions in 1955-1958 as to the future direction of development. It is frequently noted in the West that these discussions gave ample opportunities to arrive at "creative" revisionism, e.g. changes in the basic pattern of applying the Soviet model. What is NOT noted, however, is the fact that between 1955 and 1960 the Communist leaders of the region, with a few, minor exceptions, were unable to significantly differentiate themselves from the Soviet regime. With the exception of Yugoslavia and Poland -- in the latter mostly in regarding the decollectivization and land use, in the former in regards to a very wide array of activities -- the leaders of the regimes that enforced Communist rule could not make major significant changes.

It is clear that there were various -- both idiosyncratic and systemic reasons for their lack of success in developing their native -- and different! -- models. The first, and most obvious reason was the presence of Soviet power in the region. Clearly, as 1956 proved, the USSR would not allow the creation of a "free," multi-party political system that seemed to duplicate the democracy of Western political life and hence excluded the Communist parties from exercizing their monopoly over the politcal processes. Thus these regimes were certainly handicapped in trying to come up with meaningful changes that would still fall within the parameters of Soviet tolerance.

But there was a second, and perhaps even more important reason. It lay in two mutually reenforcing facts. First, the Soviet Union has selected most of the Eastern European leaders from a trained cadre whose experiences were totally within the inter-war Communist politics dominated by Moscow -- hence their total subservience to all of Moscow's dictates, real or imagined -- and second, the East European leaders knew no "other" ways or directions in which they could lead their own countries. The first fact led, after Stalin's death, to each leader vying for the dubious honor of claiming to be the "very best student of Stalin;" in Khrushchev's attack on and in his "Thaw" and his potentially dangerous liberalization drive, they saw their own position, hence their very survival, challenged. On the one hand, they were largely bewildered in trying to figure out what "safe," nationally deviationist, policies they might follow without incurring Soviet wrath or courting domestic disaster. On the other hand, however, their oppor- tunities to search for another model were equally restricted. Looking to the West in the mid-1950s, they really were unable to see great progress; Germany, their most immediate Western neighbor, still was largely in ruins, its "example" anything but shining. America and

England were far away and incomprehensible to most; France and Britain were still mired down in long colonial-type of operations. While perhaps they recognized the failures of the Soviet model -- although there is a lot of dispute on this subject -- the East European Communist leaders really had no example to draw upon that would suggest an "alternative" to the Communist developmental model.

The result of all this, to make a long and very fascinating and confusing story rather short, was that the Communist leaders in Eastern Europe really never grasped the potentialities of the "third" or "different" ways of reaching socialism. The opportunity to "mix" democratic, capitalist methods or strategies of development with those of the Soviet development in the period of the 1950s went largely unavailed for the reasons I suggested above. By 1958 the Soviets had their fill of "liberal experimentation," and in Moscow the order was given or the "suggestion" not very subtly made, that once again the Soviet model of development should be followed, especially in regards to agriculture; collectivization had to be undertaken as soon as judged feasible. Only in Poland was some limited expermentation still practiced under the watchful eyes of the USSR. And it is important to note that all -- perhaps we should charitably say nearly all -- of the East European leaders soon fell back in their role as so many "Faithful Russians" guarding the camp, once again. It was an easier role to play, of course, than that of Rabbi Low's who knew what the Golem would have wrought.

There was one, distinctly sad, aspect of this failing on the part of the Eastern European elites, one that again has gone unmentioned all too long. Implicit in the "different roads to socialism" concept was a concession from the Soviet elites to the East European elites to "reintegrate" their countries with those of the West from which Stalinist autarchism and the Iron Curtain had kept them separated. To be sure, there were to be real limits in this undertaking, as far as the Soviet elite was concerned; nonetheless, the very fact that the East European regimes could begin their own rapprochement with the West was in itself significant. When these regimes -- either through their own volition or through pressures wielded by the USSR -- once again chose the autarchic, separationist routes, when they once again realigned their countries to an even closer alliance with the USSR, they ignored the potentiality of returning to the fold of a Europe reunited.

C. The third period of Eastern European development was characterized by two contradictory trends. The first trend was the "reformist" direction; unavailed in the 1950s, in the 1960s and 1970s some of the states embarked on major domestic reforms, either initiated from below or from above, others continued to stick to

the safety of Stalinist models with minor modifications.
Although some states fluctuated between these two
extremes, the patterns of development were very clear.
The reformist states were Hungary, Poland, and reform
Czechoslovakia -- and, of course, Yugoslavia. The
"Stalinist" or centralist states were East Germany,
Romania, Bulgaria and both before and after the Dubcek
era in Czechoslovakia.

The most clearly reformist state was Hungary, where
the New Economic Mechanism of 1968, aside from the years
1972-1976, brought major decentralization of the
economy, allowed some pluralization of the political
scene and limited the control of the state over some
aspects of autonomous social development. Hungary
reincorporated some of the most important elements of
Westernism into its market, reestablished the latter's
distributive prominence, but most significantly, retied
Hungary to a Western European frame of reference and
development. Much like Yugoslavia's reform, the NEM --
though begun as a simple economic reform tool -- in
reality, was a complex mechanism to shed Hungary of most
elements of Stalinism. While remaining a "Communist"
state, Hungary, in reality, tried to become a
market-economic, state-owned, socially-operated
depoliticized country very much akin to Western Europe.

Poland, the "exceptionalist" state throughout its
existence, was also exceptional as a reform state.
Vacillating between anarchy and riots on the one hand
(1970, 1976, 1980-1982), and repression, order and
terror, on the the the other, Poland proved that Communist
states can dig their own graves by the very Communist
methods of development: through the creation of a
class-conscious and alienated proletariat that
recognizes its power. Creating this class was easy:
dealing with it was more dificult. While the Polish
reforms -- with the exception of those adopted in
1981-1982, largely due to the pressures of Solidarnosc
-- did not go as far in the direction of
decentralization as did the Hungarian NEM, in other
areas -- land ownership, workers' economic and social
rights -- they went considerably further. In fact, the
Polish reforms led to their logical conclusion; the
near-wresting of power from the hands of the Communist
party. Only the force of the Army and the ZOMO -- and it
is irrelevant in this respect whether they acted at
Soviet behest or because of "nationalistic" reasons --
reestablished the order the Soviets have demanded of
Poland's leaders. Czechoslovakia's 1968 reform plans
were similar to Hungary's NEM and Poland's "odnowy."
Dubcek's short-lived reform rule tried to combine the
concept of social renewal, economic progress, decentralization, and national development with that of
Czechoslovakia's rejoining the Western European value-
system. Ambitiously, they harked back to a concept of

political democracy, tried to invigorate a defunct and
declining economy and wished to create a social system
with a "human face" -- thereby implying that the type of
Stalinist or dictatorial system practiced by Novotny et
al, borrowed directly from the USSR, was "inhuman" and
had little or no Western values behind it, and with
which the Czechoslovaks should have no association at
all.

The rest of the Eastern European states by and large
followed the Soviet model, some successfully, others not
at all. The Soviet model of development adopted in East
Germany, though mostly preserving Soviet type institutional frameworks and normative concepts, it can be
argued, indeed, was proof that the "model" worked. The
same can be said of Bulgaria as well: though in this
case there was no large-scale assistance advanced from
the West, as in the case of East Germany, somehow the
Bulgarians did make the Soviet model a successful basis
of development.

But in other cases the Soviet model failed
miserably. Its slavish copying in Czechoslovakia failed
to make the Czech economy competitive in the world
economy or for that matter even in the socialist
economic system. Its social stagnation and the
alienation that stagnation created was phenomenal even
in Eastern Europe. In Romania, while the policy of
"entangling alliances" was clearly not based on the
Soviet model and was even frequently at odds with Soviet
desiderata, the Stalinist economic and social centralization of all aspects of life was greater even than
that the USSR exercized over its citizenry. Moreover,
the Romanian dictatorship failed to show major permanent
success for its economic policies; the huge debts to the
West notwithstanding, the Romanian economy by 1980-1982
had come to a screeching halt.

D. At the beginning of the 1980s, thus, the question
of _quo_ _vadis?_ is more relevant to ask than ever before.
Clearly, Eastern Europe has come to the edge of a new
era with choices that the leaderhsips must clearly
understand, choices that are disturbing and fraught with
danger for the elites. Nonetheless, these are clearly
choices that the elites MUST make. Faced with a world-
wide recession, with overwhelming debts, some of these
regimes face bankruptcy in the international setting.
Faced with no-growth prospects, with potential declines
and a failing scientific-technological revolution, the
elites are forced to make decisions they have postponed
all too long. Whether to decentralize or keep the
centralist model, to liberalize or keep the Stalinist
model, to Westernize or to keep the autarchic relationships within the Communist bloc forsaking other
potential ties, to strive for more independence or
greater dependence: these are options that must be
considered by the Communist leadership of Eastern

Europe. Whither Eastern Europe, thus, it must be emphasized, is NOT A QUESTION THAT DEPENDS SOLELY UPON THE INTERNATIONAL ENVIRONMENT, but also upon choices that the elites themselves must make and the rest of this paper sets out the basis on which the Eastern European leaders must make their personal calculations.

Part II. Determinants of Successes and Failures in Eastern Europe

Let us now try to observe the determinants, the parameters, in short, the variables of successes and failures in Eastern Europe. What in fact, we are trying to search for in this part of the paper is the potential "independent variable" of success and failure. Although a caveat must be entered immediately -- e.g. that the successes and failures are almost always imposed upon the systems by time-specific, nation-specific and international-environmental-specific considerations -- it seems to this observer that at least the pattern for success and failure of the policies of the Eastern European states is affected by the application of four general variables: ideological, economic (both domestic and foreign environments), political-social and international-environmental considerations.

A. My emphasis on and the inclusion of ideological variables, of course, is considered "old-fashioned" or "conservative-reactionary" by many observers today. With some justification they point out that in Eastern Europe "no one believes in ideology," that "ideology never defined a problem" or "dictated its solution." I would like to submit, however, that an approach that negates or to a major extent even diminshes the role of ideology in Eastern Europe ignores several permanent realities.

The first such permanent reality lies in the fact that Eastern European policy-makers at the top level are in their late sixties or older, and that they -- as well as their henchmen, satraps, faithful followers or subordinates -- are NO LONGER CAPABLE OF PHRASING COMPLEX, EVEN NONPOLITICAL QUESTIONS IN OTHER THAN MARXIST TERMS. Their reference point, whether one wishes to admit it or not, is not reality, but the observable reality through their own eyes, their ideological preconditioning, and their general ignorance of any other perspective that may have a relevance to solutions that can be found to complex problems is extremely limiting. Having been reared in or succeeded to power through the "general principles guiding the laws of socialist development," it is not that they believe in everything Marxist or in principles of communism writ large, but rather that they are unable to think in other terms. The debate in the West that points to the fact that Ceausescu is not a "real" Marxist, or that Kadar "really does not believe in Communism," is thus misplaced. What one must ask is what these leaders really know of the West and if they can think in terms that would allow the application of the vast knowledge that can be gained from a review of Western experience.

And in this sense, the sense of what the elites in power really know of the West, they are already at a major disadvantage. Since most of them -- aside from their native tongue and some Russian -- know no other languages, most reports published in the West reach them in translation. In what is translated for them, there exists already a screening process; reports highly favorable to the West -- in many areas of policy -- are seldom translated for them but discarded as "Western propaganda." While, perhaps, such elites know of the prosperity of the West, Western successes cannot be regarded as due to systemic determinants, anymore than Eastern European failures can be regarded in that light.

Moreover, the very language of communism is such that non-ideological considerations are very difficult to comprehend. One cannot say, for example, that "this soap does not do anything else but clean;" one must say that "this is a Communist soap, hence it is superior to a capitalist soap and thus it cleans better than any capitalist soap can." Though the example may sound absurd, for frequently there is no soap, the torturous ideology after a while becomes second nature to its practitioner who thus forgets to think in terms that are not within the reference point. Hence, one of the greatest difficulties faced by any would be reformer in Eastern Europe lies, first and foremost, in explaining that -- for instance -- a Western process of production should be adopted, in terms that are cognizant of and congruent with presumed Communist values; frequently depending upon the mental acumen, interest and comprehension of the particular leader, this is a well-nigh impossible task.

Another limitation ideology places upon the decision-makers lies in the fact that in the upward flow of decision-making process anyone higher than the individual making the report will get a "screened" or self-censored version that must include such phrases that are <u>derogatory</u> to the West and hence implicitly acknowledge the superiority of the socialist system. All such reports, thus ipso facto at best can discuss Western advances only grudgingly all the while harping on the superiority of socialism. In report after report dealing with the adaptation of Western technologies, one finds the "justification" process so strong that after a while reading these reports, it probably never occurs to most readers to question the superiority of the system: only "temporarily" or in some "selected" areas does it become obvious that some non-Communist ideas should be brought into the system.

There is one final area in which ideology is important: in assessing the bureaucratic process. As can

easily be demonstrated, the Communist system of bureau-
cratization has led to the fact that every level of
authority operates at least one step below where it
should operate. Hence, principals must deal with
class-room behavior that a teacher should deal with,
school district supervisors must deal with allocation of
teachers' free time in the schools that a principal
should deal with and so on. Thus, the absurdity in all
these systems: that because of this lack of responsibility to deal with topics that may require tough
decisions, the "buck" is passed all the way up.
Consequently, politburos are brought into decision
making on issues that should have been dealt with at far
lower levels, but have not been dealt with because of
the unwillingness of individuals to assume responsibility for decisions taken, on the one hand, and on the
other, by the very desire of upper elites to retain
decision making in their hands. Ideologically, therefore, _every_ decision assumes a potential political
coloration. One wrong decision does not mean merely
making a mistake, but can be -- and frequently is --
interpreted as an act of sabotage. Hence -- reductio ad
absurdum -- can become viewed as anti-Communist acts
intended to detract from the great struggle with the
forces of imperialism.

Thus, to what extent can we assume that the nature
of ideological adherence determines the successes or
failures of these regimes? After all, we have various
examples at hand that suggest no clear patterns. On the
one hand, we have a very pragmatic regime -- Hungary --
suggesting that the less a regime is influenced by
ideology, the more it is likely to be successful. On the
other hand, however, East Germany seems to prove that
one can be a thoroughly ideologically-oriented society
and yet register major successes. The examples of Poland
and Romania, naturally may be used to complete the
picture showing that non-adherence to ideology does not
mean success or that rigid adherence to ideology,
similarly can also result in failure.

The most, thus, that we can say at the present time
is that ideological adherence or non-adherence alone are
no guarantees for anything. Regimes, whether or not they
are rigidly adhering to ideological structures, in order
to guarantee successes, must undertake the implementation of policies that impact positively upon the
country; while the elites' perception of ideological
demands does influence the choice of policies, they seem
not to guarantee their success or their failure in and
of themselves.

B. The economic determinant or variable of successes
and failures is equally difficult to ascertain. Nonetheless, here too we can discern two basic issues of
policy development along which successes and failures
can both be measured. The first issue is the problem of

planning and centralization versus market orientation or decentralization. The second issue is the question of integration of these economies, and it concerns the problem of "autarchic-intrabloc" development versus the integration of the East European economies with that of the world.

Regarding planning and organizing the market under socialist economic circumstances, the notion of a planned and controlled mechanism ready at the service of the command economy has always been one of the key concepts of Soviet type economies. Although Marx described the centralized planning mechanism and its necessity in his Reflections on the French Revolution relatively early, it was not until the famous industrialization debates of the 1920s and the implementation of the centralized mechanism that the teleologists won the day for "total" central planning. Convinced of their righteousness by the unique evidence of meeting the first-year targets of the first Five Year Plan in the USSR -- never matched totally since! -- for Soviet economists central planning remained the cornerstone of Communist ideological-economic doctrine. Needless to say, central planning was adopted by the Eastern European elites in toto after the establishment of Communist regimes in the 1940s and served as key-word and as an organizing concept for a host of other theories.

There were, of course, several things desperately wrong with the whole concept of central planning. Lack of adequate information, slow turnaround time, inability to adjust to changing market conditions, garbage information on output, fake labor indicators, etc.; these were just merely signs of the problems with the central planning apparat and its operation. But central planning was supposed to accomplish more than an economic task: it was one more means of state control as far as the elite was concerned. Neglecting the problems of central planning, one could always point to the latter and suggest that giving up on the former was justified as a necessity of protecting state interests.

As a consequence, central planning worked relatively successfully as long as there was a surplus of labor, the possibility of engaging in the primitive accumulation of capital at the expense of labor, and, in general, expanding economies. Moreover, central planning could be seen as providing a successful answer as long as the Stalinist autarchic development pattern existed. The minute, however, when comparison with the development of the West became possible -- both through the slowly lifting Iron Curtain and the advance of communications -- the people living in centrally planned economies became aware of at least some of the failures of central planning mechanisms.

The failures of central planning as they became evident could possibily be resolved by the emergence of a mechanism that Marxist economists describe as the "secondary" -- in contradistinction to the "first," or centrally-planned -- economy. That such economies exist, of course, is not denied by any of the Communist theoreticians; what is less frequently mentioned is that the very nature of the planned economy guarantees the almost "natural" emergence of the secondary economy. While, even according to the most orthodox Marxists, the planned economy is supposed to ensure the egalitarian production and distribution elements of Communist systems, the emergence or existence of the secondary economy insures the development of societal inequalities. Thus, though central planning at least leads to grotesque malformations, it also leads to a privatization to the extent that the political elite allows individuals to fill the void created by the faults of the central plans.

For Eastern Europeans, central planning from the very beginning sounded slightly suspicious as they considered the future development of their economies. Having lived with at least some extent of state ownership and state management throughout their existence, Eastern European philosophers and economists alike mistrusted the notion of planned economies; it is not by chance, as Stalin would have said, that economic reformers such as the Yugoslav, Polish, or Hungarian economists, or the Czech reformers of 1968, were the most vocal critics of central planning; Oscar Lange, or Rezso Nyers had visions that greatly exceeded those of Yevsei Liberman both in theory and in practice.

But it was precisely in this sphere, the combination of theoretical insights relating to the criticism of the centralized system and that of the practical experience of implementing decentralizing reforms, that the greatest problems have arisen. Care had to be taken in any reform not to tackle the question of social ownership of property, not to allow "exploitation" and the non-state accumulation of surplus value in the hands of the citizenry, and not to attack the "authority" of the party in the establishment of goals and purposes of society. Inevitably, in nearly all reforms, the reformers were unable to avoid the pitfalls of politics to spill into "simple economic" questions, for only the Hungarian leadership realized that it had to depoliticize the entire system in order to proceed with economic reforms. In other words, as long as everything -- including economic decision making as well as education or literature -- could only be discussed as a political issue, economic reform was not possible.

The Prague Spring or the Polish events of 1970, 1976, or 1980-1982, thus, could not conceivably result in meaningful economic reforms and decentralization, as

long as economics wound up hostage to politcal
considerations. The genius of the Hungarian reform was
that it tackled all the sacred cows of Communist
economics -- the ownership of property, the use of
labor, egalitarian reward structure, central planning,
surplus value and exploitation, state or individual
responsibility for housing or the most flagrantly
flourishing secondary economy -- but it did so without
even discussing the right of the party in determining
the political direction for the state. Parenthetically,
though, we must add that by 1982 the Hungarian
economists also pushed for the separation of the
"sectoral" ministries as having little positive role to
play in decentralized economies. And even though both
Brezhnev and Andropov have signaled their approval of at
least some aspects of the Hungarian New Economic
Mechanism, they were hardly expected to establish
anything similar in the USSR, for in the Soviet type
systems such a "liberalization" would lead to
significant reductions of party power and there seem to
be no takers for such an act today. What the central
planning advocates hoped from the adoption ot some
lessons of the Hungarian experience is a market without
market pressures, an accurate reading of supply and
demand without price elasticity and fluctuation and
"better" incentives for production without wage
inequalities.

In addition to the debate over centralization and
decentralization, another issue also emerged slowly as
these economies developed. This issue was the question
of autarchic -- within system -- development as versus
the integration of the Communist states of Eastern
Europe with the rest of the world economy. It will be
recalled from earlier mention that by 1964 the Soviet
Union recognized the enormous costs of its own
"autarchism," both in terms of its own and that of its
allies' isolation from the world market and its rapidly
developing technologies, and the fallacy of mutual
reliance of poverty-stricken countries upon neighbors
not much more advanced. The major decisions to allow
integration with the West was made probably at the
December 1965 meeting of economic advisors to the
Comecon and those who were most eager to avail themselves to the Western markets were Hungary, Poland,
Romania, Czechoslovakia and the Soviet Union itself.
East Germany of course, was to be the beneficiary of the
internal German -- and hence to some extent the Common
-- market as well, and Czechoslovakia quickly relented
after 1968 to revert to a closed system once again. For
the Soviet Union, the size of its external trade with
the West was never to be as great as for Hungary, Poland
or Romania; nonetheless, for these four countries the
abolition of the earlier "autarchic" pattern meant
significant displacement as time went on.

Attachment to the boom cycle of Western development between the end of the 1960s and the late 1970s seemed a relatively easy task for most of these states. Sparked by the hope of quick profit and the recapturing of its "traditional" Eastern market, West Germany led the way to Western European-Soviet trade. Hiding behind the politics of Ostpolitik, there loomed a big market for Germany, a market whose appetite for everything seemed insatiable. For the West the markets of the East meant an expanding of its own boom, new jobs, lucrative capital growth, further investment opportunities and, of course, the possibility of selling surplus technologies and surplus products that were already saturated in the West. For the USSR and Eastern Europe however, trade with the West meant radically different things and brought radically different benefits.

Trade with the West for the Communist states meant, first of all, an infusion of cheap capital in the form of loans whose repayment would be prolonged far into the future. Such trade between the end of the 1960s and the beginning of the 1980s brought in nearly 100 billion dollars to the region and it alleviated much of the capital-hunger that traditionally characterized Eastern Europe. Trade, moreover, meant an infusion of technology into economies that were in sore need of such infusion. Trade meant that Western goods could be seen on the markets of the East and the people of the region could experience the advances made in their standard of living; under such circumstances food-riots would be less inevitable and scarcity would upset the population to a smaller degree than otherwise expected. Trade with the West also meant finding home for Eastern products in the hard-currency-rich countries of the West. And trade with the West meant tourism, greater communication with people from the West, and a new respectability. Oh how sweet it was to call Bucharest or Budapest the Paris of the East again!

The connection between politics and economics looks quite tenuous at this juncture to objective observers. Certainly the political atmosphere of relaxation of tensions was necessary for interbloc trade to develop; without Ostpolitik and détente such trade could not have flourished in the atmosphere that the latter needed. And certainly it is true that when the political situation turned sour -- after the Soviet occupation of Afghanistan -- the atmosphere of trade also turned sour. Sparked by the American wheat embargo, followed by other pressures on technological restrictions, the loans to the East dried up and it seemed as if politics were to be blamed for this. What most observers fail to understand, though this has been amply demonstrated, is that trade between the Eastern bloc and the West would have decreased dramatically even without the Carter embargo, the Reagan Administration's policies or the drift to anti-Soviet regimes in Britain, France and Germany, in short in all of the major industrial powers of the West.

The argument made here is that trade would have dried up anyway because it was based on one-sided and false premises as far as Eastern Europe was concerned. It was based on the Eastern European premise that loans were good, because the West would never call them, and that the West would have no recourse but to swallow hard and pump ever more money into these economies. It was false because it was assumed that any amounts paid back would be paid back in inflated dollars; and it was mistaken because it was presumed that the Eastern European economies needed the West less than the West needed the Eastern markets. All of these arguments were flawed, critically, even though the West and especially the financial institutions and governments that backed those questionable loans took a real soaking in the process. But these fallacies were not visible to Eastern European policymakers until very late in the game.

The reality of what happened to the economies of the East between 1970 and 1980 could fill the pages of many scholarly studies; suffice it here to pinpoint an area that is crucial to our concerns. As one recalls, above I have argued that the autarchist developmental theorists of the Soviet Union and the Soviet bloc argued that one had to keep the East European economies free from negative influences of Western crisis by "internal trade" arrangements only. But the great opportunities of the 1970s for tying one's economies to the West were too open and too good not to be taken for the economic policy-elites of the USSR, Poland, Hungary and Romania. While earlier sales of natural resources, semifinished and finished goods to Third World countries mostly brought in payments in political currency in the world arena, sales to the West guaranteed a hard currency influx -- an influx that became a dependence. While they were reaping the benefits of the transfer of "high technology" in every area of industry and agriculture and replacing antiquated Soviet equipment with Western models -- those benefits to be gained became a dependence. While they were reaping the benefits of cheap loans to modernize their own industry or waste those loans on riches for the elites -- the benefits of loans became a dependence on loans. And this was not a chemical dependency that could be cured "easily" by half-way souse solutions.

Thus the specter that haunted responsible economists of the East for years became a reality. The shrinking of the Western markets that would no longer accept goods deemed to be substandard when compared to Western standards, forced the states of Eastern Europe into the Third World market once again. But for most of the Third World, these goods that the East could sell were either

too expensive for the international basket cases or not
advanced enough for Kuwait or Saudi Arabia. And one
could peddle cheapish light bulbs for only so long. The
dependence on high technology and the shift to Western
machines also proved disasterous; Western machines
needed spare parts that could be had only for hard
currency; factories lay idle for the want of a two-cent
item, but the two cents could not be found in the
hard-currency poor area. And the loans had to be repaid,
not in cheap overevaluated currencies, but in under-
inflated values when the Western inflation rate in real
terms became nearly the same or lower than the interest
rates that were charged for loans. While technically it
could be argued that the East held the West in blackmail, threatening in essence to default on loans unless
interest payments were rescheduled at their behest, it
became soon clear that the lack of any new loans to
speak of, the closing of markets hitherto open to the
East halted the potential development of all of these
states midstream: in the middle of the greatest
technological change in history, the Eastern European
states are too capital-poor to invest in the industries
on which the future economies of the world will be
based.

The USSR, of course, was the least hit by the
negative influences of the end of the era; for it, trade
with the West was still "peanuts" in modern terms and
the lucrative pipeline deal once again brought a
windfall for it. But lest one forgets, for the USSR
there is a double burden: first, each year it must
import grain in an amount that is in excess of its
earnings from the natural gas pipelines to the West,
and, second, willy-nilly, Eastern Europe is still
costing them significant sums. It is clear, however,
that the economies that are nearly crippled are those of
Poland and Romania; Hungary and East Germany -- the
latter is in worse shape than Hungary if we calculate
the amount of West German indirect assistance into its
fiscal balance -- are skirting the brink, though both
are still successful in maintaining a tenuous balance on
the tightrope of economic solvency. Czechoslovakia and
Bulgaria are, of course, on the other end of the scale:
in the 1970s, not having accepted major amounts or
assistance from or trade with the West on a mutual
basis, they settled for lower levels of development than
their brethren. And although Czechoslovakia is
stagnating economically there is little chance that it
will have to become bankrupt and Bulgaria with its huge
agricultural trade speaks for itself as an example of
the autarchic success.

Thus, here too, the evidence before us regarding the
economic determinants of success or failure is scant and
confusing. The era of the 1970s saw the success of
totally decentralized systems such as Hungary and

centralized ones, such as Bulgaria. It witnessed the relative success of integration in the case of Hungary again and that of autarchy in the case of Bulgaria. It witnessed the failure of decentralization attempts in 1980 and in Poland, although it could be argued that the Poles did not go far enough in their attempts at decentralization. And it could also be argued that the 1970s witnessed the failures of development in a genuinely autarchic centralized regime: Czechoslovakia. But beyond that all we could say was that success or failure depended on the elites whose hands held the reins of policies regarding decentralization or integration in the 1970s.

    C. The third area of our examination concerns the political variable. What we are trying to ascertain is whether it made any difference -- as far as the success or the failure of the various regimes are concerned -- it a regime was "totalitarian/dictatorial" or "democratic/liberal." In my examination, obviously, I am mindful that these constructs are merely intellectual "models" whose purity, especially in being used as contradistinctive to each other, is open to question. Nonetheless, the typology is used merely to indicate the two sides of opposite positions regarding the nature of domestic rule.

    In Eastern Europe, on one side of the coin one can clearly observe the states where politics are rigidly controlled by a dictatorial party. These states -- in hierarchical order of severity of dictatorial rule -- are: Romania, Czechoslovakia, Bulgaria, and East Germany. On the other side of the coin we can list Yugoslavia, Hungary and Poland -- even today, in spite of the military rule in that country.

    Clearly, among the first group there are impressive success stories present. Economically -- even though it has a high debt service ration approaching the .50 benchmark -- East Germany has proved to be a stable, consumer-productive society, where the standard of living is still the highest among the East European states. Its products sell well in the West and the Third World markets. Moreover, the only area where there have been dysfunctions as far as the East Germans are concerned was in the area of the independent peace movement -- centered largely, though not exclusively, around the churches -- that appears to condemn nuclear armament policies, not just in the West but also in the East.

    Bulgaria also presents us with a success story. Here too, the party maintaining tight control over society squashing any opposition activities, should they miraculously emerge, has managed to maintain a stable balance. There have been no real challenges to party rule, although one often hears of murmurs of revival of nationalism and movements that were supposed to have been connected with Ludmilla Zhivkova, the late daughter of Todor Zhivkov. Like East Germany, Bulgaria has also been relatively successful in the international scene; economically, it has maintained a fine balance between relative austerity at home and the export of agricultural and selected industrial goods to the West. While its standard of living is way below that of Hungary or East Germany, there is also an absence of the incredible scarcities that exist in Poland and Romania. Bulgaria, in short -- in spite of its international stature having been sharply reduced by the Markov and Agca affairs -- managed to have weathered the crisis with its dictatorial party rule better than some of the other states.

On the other hand, we have impressive failures in existence also among the states with a dictatorial systems. Romania presents a failure of everything with the exception of the rule of the security, although even in this respect General Ion Pacepa's defection from Romania was a major blow to the system. Romania is at the edge of having to default on its loans, its program of "multilateral development" having come to a screeching halt, their MFN status withdrawn by an outraged US Congress, its treatment of nationalities and dissidents having drawn condemnation by just about every human rights group, and its international "prestige" severly damaged as the room for maneuvering among anxious superpowers narrowed. Any amount of opposition -- even if it is to the tyrannical rule of the Ceausescu nepotocracy and the whims and brutality of such members of the regime as heir apparent Niku has been noticed even in the West. Romania today is close to being a beggar state, a "sick man of Europe," whose stature is diminished by both its domestic bankruptcy and a lack of international need for its "independent brokerage" foreign policy.

Czechoslovakia is not much better off than Romania, although evidently, its domestic economic performance is slightly better than Romania's; the scarcities, so obviously everpresent in Romania's every-day life, do not exist in Czechoslovakia. Czechoslovakia, however, had had a stagnating economy, with serious drops in economic growth and while the leadership does not really seem to care if the country falls behind the West year after year both in terms of exports and imports, these failures are bound to show up. Moreover, Czechoslovakia's dictatorial rule, practiced by a Slovak controlled party elite, keeps a tight rein over the intellectuals, the Chartists and other dissidents in the country. While to date the party elites seems to have been successful in playing off the workers against the intellectuals -- the conservatives versus the liberals, if one wishes to put it that way -- in times of ever-growing economic difficulties, the party will be forced to rely to an increasing extent on the forces of the security apparat.

The examination of the liberal/democratic regimes presents once again a rather confusing picture; here, too, one witnesses successes and colossal failures side by side. The Hungarian regime presents us with impressive lists of successes. It has depoliticized public life to an extent unmatched in Eastern Europe, thus allowing the discussion and resolution of any topic concerning governance, without the potentiality of pitting the debating sides against each other as "traitors" or "defenders of true socialism." Consequently, reforms -- in the ideological and the economic sphere, in the political arena or in the intellectual camp -- could be resolved without the acrimony and hatred that characterize such behavior in other states of the region. It has managed to decentralize its economic decision-making processes, allowed greater integration with the West, begun a major program for technological importation, and through the differentiation of earning potential created a truly impressive program of rewarding individual initiative. It gave nearly free rein to the secondary economy and allowed it to dominate -- to a great extent -- over the state-controlled market, by making the market a function balancing the productive and distributive forces of society. While it has accumulated close to 10 billion dollars in medium-term loans and tried to desperately avoid rescheduling its payments to the West, it has balanced import needs necessary for further expansion with the maintenance of a relatively scarcity-free domestic consumer market. And throughout it all, it managed to keep the polity relatively happy. Although there were steps taken against the "dissidents" and "those who think differently," few people opposed to the party rule actually had been incarcerated or expelled. In fact, one of the most significant complaints against the regime on the part of a small opposition was that freedom of speech did not mean that anyone would listen to the speech of the opposition; their cries for further reforms, while muted, would not be taken seriously by the political leadership. Moreover, the regime took great care not to allow the intellectual dissidents to establish a coalition with the workers, making sure that the Polish example would not be repeated.

The Polish crisis could also be regarded as an example of mismanagement of a liberal regime on a large scale. It will be recalled that throughout the 1970s the Polish states had the most impressive freedoms granted to the population, that in all respects it was the freest country in Eastern Europe. Although it had its share of riots and _jacqueries_ in 1970 and 1976, the Polish _Solidarnosc_ movement could not have started in any other state of the region. Only in an atmosphere of furtive, beleaguered party rule, in which the leaders were unable to use force to squash the trade-unionism of the workers and unwilling to utilize the police and the army to crack down for fear of what such an action would mean in the relatively free political setting, can we explain the development of the opposition movement. But economically the Polish state, with all its decentralization and liberalism, was a travesty as far as the utilization of the large scale Western loans was concerned. The corruption among the top elite and the simple misjudgement over just about every issue of economic decision making went hand in hand and finally forced the party to the brink of the most serious social-political crisis in the nearly four decade existence of the Polish communist state. The alliance between the workers and the intelligentsia, between the party rank and file and Solidarnosc, between the workers and peasants, has brought about the crisis that finally had to be settled by a military coup. Liberalism, thus, as seen from the objective observer's point of view, was unable to create a viable reform system in either the ideological-political or the economic sub-systems and its failures, thus direcrtly contributed to the creation of the militarized regime of General Jaruzelski.

But Jaruzelski's rule was still unable to solve the country's major problems; the commissars may be able to shoot people, but they are notoriously inefficient at running factories or controlling social problems of development. Neither liberal nor dictatorial rule has been able to depoliticize public life; hence every issue remains debated from counterposed perspectives, from the perspective of "right" versus "wrong" solutions. And since the issues of development and success are not so polarized in real life, liberalism or dictatorship are not helpful constructs as determinant variables for the stability and continued growth of the Polish state.

What can we thus say about the variable of political style in examining the successes and failures of the Eastern European countries in general? It is clear that domestic political constraint and styles, once again, are not the sole determinants of successes and failures. A regime may be successful in its attempts at modernization and development regardless of the political arrangements it may have at home; the examples of Hungary and East Germany are ample proofs in this regard. Similarly, a regime may be characterized by failures, once again regardless of its domestic arrangements, as Poland and Romania seem to illustrate. Furthermore, however, if one seeks stability as the single most important regime-goal, both the liberal and the dictatorial regimes seem to have proven to be able to attain that condition: East Germany and Hungary were both stable systems, and Romania and Poland both possessed instabilities, in spite of their differences along the scale of domestic control variables.

D. Finally, let us turn to the variable of the international political environment as a determinant of Eastern European successes and failures. Seemingly, at first glance, one should disregard this measure as a valid construct; after all, all the Eastern European states prospered or failed in an environment that was similar for all of them. And yet, one cannot discard the international environment out of hand for there were several major differences that were caused by the constructs of international events.

If one examines the crucial cold-war years, until the mid-1950s, certainly, all the Eastern European states had been equally affected by both the Soviet Union and the West dealing with them as mere extensions of the USSR. By the early 1960s, however, there began a cautious differentiation both among the local elites as they carved out different destinies for their own countries, as well as on the part of Moscow as to which countries were urged to turn in certain directions.

Regarding the choices open to East European elites, the question of choice has frequently been played down by many observers. It is largely a matter of faith that Eastern European elites are simply "told" what needs to be done and they would "slavishly follow Soviet wishes." This matter, of course, is far more complex than it appears at first glance. After all, it is true that in important matters, frequently, the Eastern European elites are presented with a simple diktat by the Soviet "masters;" witness for instance the treatment meted out to Czechoslovakia's reformist leaders in Moscow after August 21, 1968. But most frequently even Soviet desiderata is couched in terms that are "nicer" or "more polite" when such demands are presented, especially to first secretaries of the various parties. The very nature of the ideological setting, in which the "Communist commonwealth" operates, in which the various first secretaries are viewed as the legitimate leaders of the countries which they represent, argues for a respect by the Soviet leaders -- even if in private or behind the back of certain figures many a Soviet leader makes nasty and mean, though often much too true, snide remarks. Moreover, it is also clear that there is the element of choice available to each elite, even if it is not a "total" choice. There is ample evidence around that the extent of implementation of certain decisions is left largely open. The Husak leadership's open avowal of their desire of trying to fulfill Soviet desiderata, versus the Hungarian leaders' desire to "get around" many Soviet wishes is merely one illustration of this complex relationship, but indirect behavioral evidences also abound.

124

Nonetheless, it is clear that there was considerable leeway given to the Romanian leadership in its efforts to find a "third" road, one that would keep them in the Comecon and the Warsaw Pact, but also one that would help them act as a go-between both in the cases of the Chinese-Soviet as well as the Soviet-American conflicts, especially in the latter case as that confrontation related to the Middle East. While parameters of these independent policies clearly changed over time -- with the Romanians taking greater and greater "liberties" as far as the Soviets were concerned -- these limits always existed in a relatively well-defined manner. Thus the Romanians were allowed to seek a greater cooperation with Yugoslavia, but they were not allowed to propose or accept any sort of a "confederation" with the latter. Thus, for instance, while the USSR did not like the Romanian support of policies that condemned Soviet actions in Afghanistan, they did not specifically or officially prohibit that support to the Romanians. On the other hand, the Soviet ambassador to the United Nations, in the latter instance, told the Romanian ambassador to the United Nations that Romania would "not be in a position" to vote condemning the USSR's invasion of Afghanistan: hence the curious "abstention" of Romania on the issue in the General Assembly after the strong and vocal support of such condemnation in the earlier debate.

It is, of course, also clear that elements of choice were important for the national Communist leaders as well, and that they were cognizant of the existence of these opportunities. In 1968, the Czechoslovak leadership, for instance, "restrained" those elements within the elite that sought "closer" ties with West Germany. In Poland, even the supporters of the reform leadership in 1981-1982 were always very careful not to give an anti-Soviet hue to the reform movement, lest the USSR would be more unduly imbued with anxiety than it was as a result of the internal turmoil in Poland.

And there were real "transgressions" as well. The most notable such transgression was, of course, the withdrawal of Hungary from the Warsaw Pact in 1956, even if such a transgression had taken place AFTER the Soviet invasions of Hungary began for the second time. But other, less dramatic transgressions have also taken place, ranging from the original Czechoslovak acceptance of the Marshall Plan to the sometimes purposive transshipment of Soviet goods, destined for Eastern Europe, to the West. All of these examples are simple illustrations, however, of the fact that even in foreign policy, some leeway and choice was always implicit for the East European leaders in their roles as the representatives of their respective states.

In the international environment of the late 1960s and early 1970s, international issues took on a largely

economic hue. Romania, Poland and Hungary all sought an
increase in trade and contact with the Western European
states and -- evidently as far as the Soviet leadership
was concerned -- that was ok for them. Intra-German ties
also moved in the same direction, after Khrushchev's
last ill-fated attempt to dictate a German-Allied-Soviet
settlement. That Bulgaria or Czechoslovakia chose not
to avail themselves to great increases in Eastern
European-Western ties -- again as far as the Soviet
leadership was concerned -- was their business.

Many analysts, of course, argue of the primacy of
economic considerations in East-West ties; I would like
to suggest that politics played just as much, if not an
even greater role. For ties with the West, especially
with the United States and the World Bank, implied an
opening of the respective states to the West, its trade,
its contact and its influence. But the extent of opening
was different in each case. For Romania with its tight
Stalinist regime, the opening was limited to "the
family," to those selected to deal with the West, and
every effort was made to limit Western influence
strictly to the economic sphere. For Poland and Hungary,
the US' MFN treatment and the precious ties to the West
also mean an at least "partial" rejoining of the West,
being a part of the Western processes whether one
"liked" them or not.

But the impact of political changes were also
noticeable after the end of the era of détente and the
imposition of restrictions that began to harm Eastern
European economic stability. Even, as I argued above, if
the Western trade with the East was bound to decrease as
the West entered the "bust" cycle of economic development, the political atmosphere also seriously
deteriorated those already fragile relationships. The
response to the invasion of Afghanistan was a convenient
way of signaling to the East, the Polish debacle a real
shocker, and it must be argued, that viewed in this
context, Romania's introduction of the exit tax -- which
otherwise would have been somehow explained away by a
State Department anxious to maintain good relations with
"the enemy of my enemy" -- in the international
environment of the 1980s was viewed as a sharp signal of
initiating a response of "not an inch further." At the
mid-point of the Reagan Administration, thus, it looks
like Hungary is the sole country in Eastern Europe being
able to maintain good and friendly relations with the
United States and the Western community as a whole.

What can we conclude, thus, of the international
environment as a variable of successes and failures?
Once again, the data show countervening trends. For
some, like Hungary, Poland or Romania, beneficial trends
in international politics were tools to be utilized,
while for others, it was thought that one did not really
need favorable winds to trade on a minimal level. For

Hungary, ties with the West were far too important to be
neglected by a negative development in international
relations: the crackdown on dissidents, begun after
Andropov's accession, seized as soon as the Western
response began to spill over into the economic sphere.
For Poland, too, the impact of the international
environment has been driven home with a really negative
message: the Polish leaders realized that there would be
no improvement in international economic activities,
improvements that Poland sorely needed, until there was
a marked improvement in the international political
climate and that was not likely to occur until the end
of military rule was not in sight. Thus, the
international environment alone, certainly, could not be
used as an independent variable of successes and
failures, but that it did impact upon them -- both
negatively and positively, both by choice and by
accident -- is quite clear.

In closing this paper, I think it is important to
summarize what I hope is evident from the above
discussion, namely that none of the above variables --
the ideological, economic, political or the international environmental variables -- can be considered to
be "independent," that when used alone, none of them can
explain the successes and failures of the Eastern
European states. While this conclusion is hardly
stunning, it should cause us to pause in our
generalizations for a brief moment. For if my
conclusions are correct, then one can only claim that
the skill, ability and talents of the individual
leaders, and/or if one wishes, the "national character"
of the people of the region are more important
indicators of the success and failure of these regimes,
than are the "systemic" variables we so closely
associate with the crisis of Eastern Europe. Viewed in
this light, the failures of a Husak, a Jaruzelski, a
Ceausescu or the dozens of other has-been figures of
Eastern European history that have come and gone during
the last few decades, are just as stunning as the
successes of a Kadar, or of a Honecker. And viewed in
this light, the native desire of the Germans to work and
the enormous work of the Hungarian people especially for
the improvement of their own lot, suggests that as long
as the rest of the Eastern European leaders do not allow
their people to reap personal benefits from the system
through whatever means, these states will not be able to
get out of the crisis. And for the Soviet and Eastern
European leaders the last lesson is now driven home with
a force never before recognized. Whether they will take
these lessons and attempt to correct the mistakes that
have led these states to near bankruptcy, of course, is
anybody's guess, and ultimately it is their own
business. And just as those leaders before them who have
bit the dustbin of history -- Rakosi, Novotny, Gomulka

or Gierek -- the present leaders, if they are not lucky enough to pass on before it happens, will have to answer to the people whom essentially they and the Communist system alike have failed in their quest for a better future.

7. Observations on Trends in East-West Trade in the 1970s

J. Michael Montias

Introduction

In the last decade, Soviet and East European economic growth and trade have been affected, to an extent unprecedented since World War II, by the repurcussions of events that occured outside the CMEA area. The OPEC-initiated increases in energy prices that buffeted the world's economy from 1973 to 1980 have by now more or less been digested in the East. But they are still having an indirect impact on the socialist economies since the Soviet Union, which shielded its allies from the initial shock, has been gradually raising the prices of its exported oil to world levels. The deterioration in the terms of trade of the East European importers of Soviet oil continues to exert a depressing effect on their growth. The downward trend in East European growth rates, which has been fairly steady since 1976, would have started two or three years earlier if it were not for another exogenous event that was indirectly linked to the rise in oil prices. In 1974 and 1975 the hugely swollen earnings of the OPEC members deposited in Western banks created a pool of loanable funds that became available at initially attractive rates to industrializing nations both in West and East. These recycled petrodollars helped to sustain high rates of growth in several East European economies, including especially Poland and Romania. Eventually, though, the nations that had drawn most deeply on these Western loans suffered the most severe setbacks when it came time to repay them at higher interest rates and they had to sell their exports on the depressed and increasingly protectionist Western markets of the early 1980s. The socialist economies had much the same experience as the newly industrialized nations which borrowed heavily in the mid-1970s and fell into payment difficulties a few years later. The similarity of the experiences should not obscure the fact that CMEA members accumulated a much smaller volume of debt than the newly industrializing nations. Their total indebtedness, exclusive of the Soviet Union, only came to $53 billion in 1982 ($480 per capita) compared to $84 billion for Brazil ($650 per capita) and $80 billion for Mexico ($1,100 per capita). The notoriety of Poland's and Romania's virtual defaults should not cause us to overlook the fact that all the other European CMEA members including the Soviet Union have managed to keep their external debt under effective control, and even to reduce its absolute size in the last year or two.

This chapter attempts to sort out, in a preliminary and tentative way, external and internal factors in the Soviet and East European area's hochkonjunktur of 1970-1975 and in the downswing and stagnation of the last seven years. Along the way I will describe some of the main trends in recent East-West trade, comment on the competition between Eastern Europe and the newly industrializng nations in Western markets, and speculate on political aspects of Western restrictions on machinery exports to CMEA.

Interdependence

In the second half of the 1960s, neither the East European states nor the Soviet Union seemed interested in securing Western loans. Czechoslovakia's negotiations for a large West German loan in the summer of 1968 was a short-lived exception, squashed by the Soviet invasion in August of that year. Gomulka's Poland reduced its indebtedness in this period to a negligible magnitude. The Bulgarians had engaged in fairly heavy borrowing in the first half of the 1960s. Having later had considerable difficulty in servicing their debt, they were loath to go back to the well; the Soviet Union, which is said to have bailed Bulgaria out with a gold loan, firmed up its ally's resolve not to engage for some time in such risky ventures. As late as 1971, the total indebtedness of Eastern Europe was only $6 billion, of which only about 50 percent was commercial bank credit and the rest government-secured loans.

What caused the Soviet and East European leaders to engage in large-scale borrowing starting about 1971? Détente, the Helsinki spirit, the securing of Soviet and Polish postwar territorial gains at the expense of Germany surely were all bound up with the political decision taken by the ruling Communist parties to open their countries to trade and credit. But these decisions would not have been taken had there not been a compelling desire to forestall a slowdown in the pace of economic growth that was threatening the area. In the case of Poland, growth had already begun to wind down appreciably in the 1960s -- in part owing to lower accretions to the labor force -- and there seemed to be no other way to combine high rates of capital formation and socially tolerable increases in real incomes than to draw on external sources to propel the economy foreward. That Western banks were then awash in petro-dollars for

which they were eager to find lending opportunities was
a felicitous coincidence. It was especially advantageous
to the East because, as a result of the Western
recession of 1974-1975 triggered off by the OPEC-ordered
increases in oil prices, the Western demand for bank
credit had abated and more credit was available for
lending to CMEA countries than would otherwise have been
the case. The symbiotic relation between East and West
during these years had another dimension. It will be
recalled that there was no recession in the Soviet Union
or Eastern Europe at this time. (No doubt there would
have been a recession in the energy-poor countries of
the region, including especially Czechoslovakia, the GDR
and Hungary, if the Soviet Union had not spared them
from the full impact of higher energy costs by keeping a
lid on the prices of its oil deliveries in 1974 and then
in raising its prices only gradually in subsequent
years.) The continued strength of machinery and
equipment purchases by the socialist countries in 1974
and 1975 helped many high-technology Western suppliers
to weather the recession. In this instance East-West
trade acted countercyclically.

The 1974-1975 experience was in marked contrast to
what happened in 1981-1982 when the Western recession
was aggravated by a sharp drop in machinery and
equipment orders from the East, caused in turn by the
stagnation or decline of investments througout Eastern
Europe.[2] On this occasion, the Soviet Union still
behaved countercyclically, as its gross fixed investments and its imports from the West continued to
increase, albeit at a declining rate. Nonetheless,
Western exports to CMEA as a whole, even after factoring
in the drop in the world-market prices of these last two
years, were still slightly below 1980 levels in
September 1982.[3] In the next few years, Eastern Europe's
terms of trade with the Soviet Union will continue to
worsen, due to the upward movement in Soviet export
prices propelled by the five-year moving average of
world prices. CMEA oil prices will not reach their peak
until at least 1984 (unless the moving-average formula
is corrected). The East European economies will
presumably have little foreign exchange to spare to
increase their imports of Western manufactures. Only the
strength of Soviet imports, which amounted in 1981 to
about 60 percent of total European CMEA imports of
semifabricated and manufactured goods from the West, is
likely to keep shoring up the demand for these goods.

Soviet Strategic Considerations

We have just seen that Soviet price policy
critically influenced Eastern Europe's trade in
manufactures with the developed West. Other Soviet
decisions affect trade with the Third World. To the
extent that the Soviets cannot or will not satisfy their

CMEA partners' demands for raw materials, and especially
for crude oil, the East European states must buy these
materials from developing countries at higher prices.
The bulk of Eastern Europe's trade with these countries
is centered on Iraq, Libya, Syria, and Iran which supply
the CMEA Six (Bulgaria, Czechoslovakia, the GDR,
Hungary, Poland, and Romania) with oil in exchange for
manufactures, a large part of which consists of
armaments.[4] Soviet policy also constrains the volume and
structure of East European exports to the West by
preempting some of the most technologically up to date
equipment produced by its more advanced CMEA partners.
An influential East German scholar in a recent interview
with an American public figure avowed that the post-
Brezhnev Soviet administration was even more demanding
than the old in this respect: the best optical
instruments must be sold to Eastern rather than Western
buyers.[5] It is not clear whether the Soviets just want
to apply these high-tech items for their own industrial
or military ends or whether they are also concerned lest
they fall into the hands of Western users. Even though
the (legal and illegal) trade in strategic items goes
mainly from West to East, there is a growing potential
in the GDR and Czechoslovakia for a reverse flow.

Strategic considerations play a significant role in
"industrial policy," which may be defined as the
selection of branches of industry that, in the eyes of
the planning authorities, deserve to be promoted for the
contribution they can make to a country's export program
or to its technological potential, or for other pregnant
reasons. Both in 1947-48 and in 1967-68 prominent
Czechoslovak economists advocated a policy of export
specialization geared primarily to advanced engineering
products that could be sold for hard currency in the
West. Their views were rejected by the official
proponents of "CMEA preference" -- the necessity of
giving priority to the requirements of other CMEA
members. The Soviet invasion of 1968 put an end to the
discussion. In the case of Poland the failure to
implement an efficient program of industrial specialization geared to hard-currency exports in the late
1960s -- a program that Gomulka himself was eager to go
forward with -- may in part be traced to resistance
emanating from the military establishment. The military
were apparently reluctant to allow the curtailment of
less efficient branches of industry that would have lost
out in the competition for resources if[6] export-oriented
industries had been given high priority.

Western Strategic Interests

There is no agreement on the economic impact of
Western machinery and equipment exports to the Soviet
Union or to Eastern Europe. These imports, valued in

domestic rubles, make up a small fraction of total investments. Yet they may in certain cases widen bottlenecks and solve technological problems that could not otherwise be mastered. Multivariate analysis applied to constant-elasticity-of-substitution-production functions must cope with very difficult econometric problems to measure, with any degree of reliability, the differential effect of these imports on aggregate productivity.[7] The lengths to which the Soviets are willing to go and the expenses they are willing to sustain to obtain equipment on the COCOM list may provide better indicators of the marginal value productivity of these inputs, as they perceive them, than any we can derive from the statistical analysis of production functions.

Another aspect of the problem requiring further study is the dependence of CMEA exports to the West on high-tech imports from the West. Polish ships could not be exported to Western Europe if it were not for the advanced components (e.g. gyroscopes) imported from advanced market economies that they incorporate. The high-quality steel imports needed to meet the high standards of exported machine tools also play a role here. The attempt of countries such as Poland and Romania to solve their balance of payments problems with hard-currency economies by cutting down on their imports from the West are likely to run into one form or another of this mutual interdependence.

Whatever may be the precise impact on Soviet productivity and growth of Western equipment imports, it is perceived rather differently in Europe and the United States. European analysts tend to belittle it, Americans -- especially in the U.S. Department of Defense -- to magnify it. This was surely evident during the public debate on the pros and cons of prohibiting the exports of General Electric compressors for installation in the Soviet gas pipeline. Perceptions, however, may be affected by self-interest. It is understandable that the European nations, which have the highest stake in trade with the East, should be the ones with the greatest interest in preserving it. The Soviet Union and Eastern Europe buy 3.5 percent of France's total exports of machinery and equipment and nearly 4 percent of the Federal Republic's (18 percent of total machine-tools exports in 1980), but less than 0.5 percent of the United States' exports in this general category (SITC 7). Germany contributed 45 percent of the total NATO alliance's exports of machinery and equipment to the Soviet Union and 43 percent of NATO exports to CMEA as a whole. The respective figures for France were 18 and 17 percent, for the United States 8 and 6 percent. These percentages were in striking contrast to the shares of these three nations in total NATO defense expenditures:

134

12 percent for the Federal Republic, 9 percent cent for France, and 56.5 percent for the United States (all in 1979).[8]

Wherever a nation's share in the total defense expenditures of the NATO alliance is much smaller than its share of machinery and equipment exports to the Soviet bloc, it is apt to treat the contribution of its exports to the strengthening of the Warsaw Pact nations' military potential as an "externality." In other words, it will consider its own contribution to any putative increment in Soviet and East Europen military power too small to take into account in setting the level of its own defense expenditures. This is certainly not the case for the United States, which carries over half the total burden and must therefore "internalize" the military consequences of its strategic exports. Collective security is a public good. When one nation bears much of the burden, there is always a temptation for others to become "free riders." Neutral nations like Austria and Switzerland, which do not contribute to NATO at all, are even less likely to take into account the contribution they make to Soviet defense capabilities by their exports of strategic goods. Interestingly enough, the share of CMEA members in Austria's exports of machinery and equipment is nearly three times as high as the Federal Republic's (11 versus 4 percent in 1980). In absolute value these Austrian exports came to $563 million, or about two thirds of the country's total defense expenditures, which amounted to $857 million in 1979. The Federal Republic's exports of machinery and equipment to CMEA came to only one tenth of her defense expenditures. The comparable ratio for the United States -- 0.4 percent -- was still more minute. It is not surprising that the contribution that exports to CMEA can make to the alleviation of domestic employment problems weighs more heavily in some Western policy makers' decisions than the impact of these exports on the Soviets' defense capabilities.

CMEA Competition with the Third World on Western Markets

At several points I have mentioned that the CMEA Six (and to a much lesser extent the Soviet Union) have had some success in the last decade in increasing their exports of manufactures to the West. They have done so in part with the help of imported licenses and by importing key components and high-quality materials that they could not themselves produce. The more advanced CMEA members -- Czechoslovakia and the GDR -- already achieved a structure of exports to OECD countries dominated by manufactures by the late 1960s. The greatest structural changes occured in Poland and Hungary. In Poland the share of manufactured goods (SITC 5 to 8) in exports to the West increased from 36.5

percent in 1970 to 50.1 percent in 1981. In Hungary the increase was from 42.3 to 59.9 percent. The less developed CMEA members have been especially successful in raising the share of machinery and equipment in their exports to OECD countries. In Poland this share rose from 2.5 percent in 1965 to 13.9 percent in 1980, in Hungary from 4.3 to 12.7 percent between the same two years, in Romania from 0.7 to 7.7 percent, in Bulgaria from 1.9 to 9.2 percent. By contrast, the comparable shares for GDR and Czechoslovakia starting from a higher level, declined slightly (from 21.8 to 19.5 percent for the former and from 16.4 to 13.9 percent for the latter).[9] Such successes as the socialist countries have registered in increasing their manufactured exports to the West have been eclipsed by the extraordinary performance of newly industrializing nations, including principally Argentina, Brazil, Mexico, South Korea,[10] Taiwan, Singapore, Hong Kong, Portugal and Spain.

Consider first the relative performances of CMEA and the newly industrialized countries (NICs) in machinery and transportation equipment exports on OECD markets. In 1965 CMEA sold more than tenfold as much of these goods to OECD nations as did the NICs -- $158 million versus $12-13 million. In 1980 CMEA sold $2.3 billion on this market, the NICs $12.8 billion. The ratio was now 5.5 times to 1 in the NICs' favor. CMEA's share of OECD imports of machines and transportation equipment was 0.1 percent in 1970 and 0.7 percent in 1980; the NIC's share increased from 0.1 percent in 1970 to 4.1 percent in 1980. Among the CMEA countries, the GDR had the highest share of machinery and transportation equipment -- 19.5 percent in 1980 -- in its exports to the OECD market. The comparable shares for Singapore and Taiwan were 36.7 and 24.0 percent respectively.[11] While there was some overlap in the machinery products sold by both groups of countries, it would appear that the NICs concentrated on electric and electronic products, the CMEA exporters on machine-tools and other non-electric machinery.

Two areas where CMEA and the NICs have been competing directly are shipbuilding and automotive exports. The shipbuilding industries of South Korea, Singapore, and Brazil, which were of negligible importance in the late 1960s have grown by leaps and bounds with the help of U.S. and Japanese licenses. They have now become a serious threat to Eastern Europe's exporters. In 1970, for instance, Eastern Europe exported ships valued at $406.6 million, while the NICs exported only $33.6 million. In 1979, Poland and East Germany, the principal exporters, marketed ships for about $1 billion, compared to nearly $2 billion for the NICs (principally Brazil, Mexico, South Korea, and Singapore).[12] Since in recent years the Soviet Union, which has been the traditional market for Polish and East German ships, has been buying a significant proportion of its shipbuilding imports from the NICs, competetion between East and South has become increasingly sharp in both Eastern and Western markets.

The production of automobiles increased rapidly in the Soviet Union and Poland (coproduction with Fiat) and in Romania (coproduction with Renault) in the 1970s. No significant progress was made in this area in the GDR or Czechoslovakia. Among the NICs, Brazil, South Korea, and Spain were powerful newcomers in the field. NICs' exports of cars, measured in dollar terms, were a fraction of Eastern Europe's in 1970; they had outstripped their socialist competitors by the end of the decade. Spain alone exported nearly as much as CMEA as a whole (and two to three times as much as CMEA on the OECD market alone).[13] Brazil's exports of cars first exceeded Poland's and Czechoslovakia's in 1978. By the early 1980s it had already forged way ahead of its East European competitors. If we except Spain, the NICs' most spectacular progress has been in exports of internal-combustion engines and automobile parts rather than in exports of the finished products. Exports of engines and parts to OECD countries by Brazil and Mexico (mostly to the US), totaled about $740 million in 1980, compared to $153 million for CMEA as a whole.[14] It may be expected that these two NICs, which directed a large share of their exports of cars and engines to other Latin American countries in the 1970s, will focus increasingly on OECD markets in the 1980s, in direct competition with the Soviet Union and Eastern Europe.

Similar stories can be told for steel and synthetic fibers, two other industries where the exports of CMEA members and NICs overlap. In the case of steel, it may be noted that Eastern Europe imports quality (chiefly alloy) steels and exports, for the most part, inexpensive carbon steels, whereas Brazil and South Korea, two of the most dynamic steel exporters among the NICs, export and import steels of less disparate unit values.

Most of the successful forays of the NICs on world markets have been facilitated by access, through co-production arrangements and licenses, to the technology of the world's most powerful multinational enterprises. Eastern Europe has not profited to nearly the same extent from this flow of high technology from more to less advanced countries. Poland and Romania, which did engage in joint ventures with Western firms on a fairly significant scale, are now retreating from this policy, owing in part to their acute balance-of-payments problems with hard-currency countries.

The extraordinary production and export record of the NICs in the last decade has been marred by growing debts to US and European banks, the inability to repay which threatens the stability of the Western monetary system. Some data on the gross indebtedness of these

borrowers was cited in the introduction. The net
indebtedness to commercial banks of Mexico, Brazil, and
Argentina amounted to about $100 billion in 1980, or at
least twice as much as the CMEA as a whole. Even per
capita the commercial debts of the three NICs have
significantly exceeded those of Poland and Romania. All
five countries borrowed when abundant credit was
available at low rates of interest (8-9 percent) and
were unable to meet their repayment schedules when
interest rates rose above 12 percent while their export
earnings were adversely affected by the Western
recession of 1980-81. As is well-known, Poland's
troubles were aggravated by a succession of poor
harvests and by irresistible internal pressures for
higher food consumption both before and during the
Solidarity period. All five countries had very high
rates of investment in the 1970s. In the period 1978-80,
their "overheated" economies could not be restructured
fast enough to generate the current-account surpluses in
their balance of payments that would have been necessary
to service their debts successfully. The problems faced
by the five debtor nations, whether they were centrally
planned or primarily market-oriented, were similar in
many respects. It is not surprising that the Soviet
Union, which benefited from windfall gains in its terms
of trade and was a prudent borrower to begin with, was
able to manage its debt successfully. It is more
remarkable that Hungary, whose net commercial indebtedness amounted to $559 per capita in 1980 (nearly as
much as Mexico's), was also able to keep its debt under
control, despite a continuing deterioration in its terms
of trade. (A hard-currency liquidity crisis was averted
in March 1982 by a combination of cuts in imports and a
boost in exports.) I think we may tentatively conclude
from this comparative experience that both centrally
planned and market economies are vulnerable to
debt-management crises and that their ability to
overcome them depends more on whether they can implement
the painful policies necessary to restore equilibrium in
their domestic and external markets than on the nature
of their economic systems.

Prospects for East-West Trade
The hochkonjunktur in East-West trade of the early
to mid-1970s was brought about by a combination of
circumstances that are very unlikely to occur in the
1980s: 1) very high rates of investment in most CMEA
countries; 2) a willingness to import a large proportion
of the invested machinery and equipment from the West to
accelerate technical progress and modernize domestic
industry; 3) buoyant demand for CMEA exports on Western
markets and a high availability of credit at moderate
interest rates making it possible for Eastern buyers to
finance their purchases from the West; 4) Soviet

deliveries of oil and other raw materials at prices that did not increase nearly as much as they did on world markets. The plans for 1981-85 call for significantly lower increases in gross investment throughout the CMEA area than the plans for 1976-80, which, for the most part, were not fulfilled in this area. Gross investment is slated to decrease in Czechoslovakia and Poland, to remain at 1980 levels in Hungary, and to increase by only 0.5 percent per year in the GDR. In Bulgaria and Romania, countries notorious for their teleological planning, they were expected to rise at 3.6 and 5.2 percent per year respectively, but the declines registered in 1982 (11 percent in Bulgaria and 2.5 percent in Romania) make it very doubtful that the long-term average can be achieved. Even the moderate rise planned in the Soviet Union (2.3 percent over period 1981-85) is placed in doubt by the stagnation in investments of the last two years.

What share will Western suppliers of machinery and equipment have in these very slowly rising investments? Probably not nearly so high as in the past, both by reason of the more acute balance-of-payments problems faced by most CMEA members, compared to the mid-1970s, and of the deterioration in the political climate and in the economic relations between East and West. The East having made a brave attempt to open itself to trade and credits in the 1970s and having suffered the unintended consequences of this policy is doubtlessly moving into a period of bloc-wide relative autarchy. Increasingly stringent NATO controls on strategic exports to CMEA members will encourage their inward-turning policy. Western recovery from the deep recession of 1981-82 will presumably help to sustain higher levels of East-West trade than in the recent trough years, but Western banks will not provide the loans -- assuming the socialist states were desirous of obtaining them -- that would be necessary to propel trade to higher levels.

The ability of the East European members of CMEA to earn hard currencies will undoubtedly be adversely affected by the continued progress of the NICs in penetrating Western markets. The further deterioration in the terms of trade of the energy-poor CMEA members (as Soviet energy prices are gradually raised to world market levels) will force them to export more of their available surpluses to the Soviet Union; as a result they will have even less hard currency to buy from the developed West than the would otherwise have had. The rise in energy prices will also reinforce Soviet pressure on the GDR and Czechoslovakia to earmark their best high-technology goods for the Soviet market.

I cannot escape the conclusion that the only realistic prospect of significantly increasing the trade of CMEA members with external partners lies in the field of armaments. Unless tensions in the Middle East and

Central America subside in the near future, there will be favorable opportunities for CMEA armaments exports to these troubled areas. In the case of the Middle East at least, exports of "special machinery items" can be offset by purchases of oil products (to the extent that they are paid for at all). This mutually advantageous trade has its own limits: for the more armaments are brought into the area, the greater are the chances that war will spread from the Persian Gulf to the other countries of the region, which would necessarily entail a curtailment in oil production and exports. Irrespective of this dire conclusion, one might wish that the growth of East-West trade would rest henceforward on more solid grounds, consonant with the inherent complementarities between the resource endowments of Eastern Europe and the advanced market economies and the possibilities for an energizing flow of modern technology for the production of non-strategic goods from the world's technolgocial leaders to the socialist nations.

NOTES

1. Wharton Economic Forecasting Associates, "Centrally Planned Economies: Current Analysis," 1983, vol. 3, no. 20-21, p. 16.
2. Gross fixed capital formation decreased in both 1981 and 1982 in Czechoslovakia, Hungary, Poland and Romania. In Bulgaria and the GDR, the 1982 decline more than offset the increases registered in 1981. These data are culled from the U.N. Economic Commission for Europe's Economic Survey of Europe in 1982, New York, 1983, vol. 2, pp. 152-3.
3. Ibid, p. 351.
4. Wharton Econometric Forecasting Associates point out that the bulk of Czechoslovak exports to Libya, Iraq, and Syria consist of "machinery and appliances not elsewhere specified," a code name for armaments ("Centrally Planned Economies; Current Analysis," vol. 3, no. 26, p. 3).
5. Confidential interview.
6. I set forth this conjecture in my paper, "Industrial Policy in Eastern Europe: The Polish Experience," I.S.P.S. Working Paper #1006, New Haven, May 1983.

7. For a discussion of the technical problems involved, see Yasushi Toda, "Technology Transfer to the USSR: The Marginal Productivity Differential and the Elasticity of Intra-Capital Substitution in Soviet Industry," Journal of Comparative Economics, vol. 3, June 1979, 181-194.

8. The source is United Nations, Bulletin on World Trade in Engineering Products 1980, New York, 1982, for defense expenditure data, it is The International Institute for Strategic Studies' The Military Balance 1979-80, London, 1979.

9. All the above data are reproduced from Kazimierz Poznanski's "New Dimension in International Trade: East South Competition in the West," unpublished manuscript, December 1982, p. 17 and Table 3.

10. The competition between CMEA and the newly industrializing nations on Western markests is analyzed in Poznanski's study (cited above) and in Eva Palocz-Nemeth's "Der Handel in Industriewaren Zwischen Ost, West, und Süd und seine Auswirkungen," Forschungsberichte, No. 67, 1981, Wiener Institut für Internationale Wirtschaftsvergleiche.

11. Poznanski, op. cit. pp. 17-19.

12. Poznanski, op. cit. Table 12.

13. Poznanski, op. cit. Table 14.

14. Poznanski, op. cit. Table 15.

8. East-West Economic Relations: An East-West or a West-West Problem?

Angela E. Stent

Although East-West economic relations remain primarily an East-West issue, they have recently become more of a West-West problem. This is because US and European policies on East-West commercial relations have increasingly diverged over the last few years, and East-West trade has become a major source of conflict between America and her allies to the detriment of NATO's security. Indeed, East-West trade -- while economically only of limited significance for any Western economy -- has been elevated to an issue of transatlantic political controversy totally disproportionate to its economic value. Moreover, contrasting US and European views on East-West trade reflect far deeper transatlantic differences over how to interpret and respond to the Soviet challenge.

This brief paper will discuss two aspects of East-West trade as an alliance problem -- the difference between US and European definitions of security and contrasting American and European views on the linkage between politics and economics.

Security -- US and European Views

The US has traditionally viewed East-West economic relations as essentially political, disproportionately beneficial to the Soviet Union and morally questionable. Despite America's economic problems, East-West non-agricultural trade is not perceived to bring any economic advantages, but to act to the detriment of US security. Indeed, the US has never resolved an inherent contradiction in its attitudes toward East-West trade; the conflict between political/military and economic security. US policy has fluctuated between emphasising the need to restrict economic relations with the USSR for national security reasons and the desirability of promoting exports to the East to help the American economy. When in doubt, political considerations have always prevailed over economic ones.

By contrast, Europeans view East-West commercial ties as a normal, desirable element in their relations

with Comecon countries, for both politcal and economic
reasons. The major debate over East-West commercial
relations in Europe appears to focus not on what one
should sell to the East, but on how to deal with the US
on these questions. There is, of course, a basic
economic reason for the European interest in commercial
relations with Comecon. European economies are far more
trade-dependent than is the US economy, and in times of
high unemployment, East-West trade appears to be a
stable guarantee for export markets. Indeed, political
parties in all parts of the political spectrum share
this consensus. In the Federal Republic of Germany, for
instance, the CDU-CSU is as interested in trade with the
East as is the SPD.

As a result of differing economic interests,
geographical locations and historical interactions with
Eastern Euorpe, the US and its allies do not share the
same definition of security. The American concept of
security is overwhelmingly military in nature, whereas
that espoused by the Europeans is equally economic.
Moreover, to the extent that the allies agree that
high-technology exports pose a military threat to the
security of the West, they disagree on where to draw the
line. Europeans agree with the US on the need to control
exports that have a <u>direct</u> application to actual Soviet
military power, that is, items that could be diverted to
actual use in the conduct of war. But Washington has
recently broadened its definition of security controls
to include goods and technologies that contribute
<u>indirectly</u> to the conduct of war -- namely exports that
serve to strengthen the entire Soviet industrial base.
One reason why the US and its allies are in conflict
over East-West trade is because the US has a narrower
definition of what contributes to national security and
a broader definition of what threatens it than do the
Europeans.

The latest examples of these disagreements involve
the Soviet pipeline. The dispute between the US and its
allies over the construction of the West Siberian
natural gas pipeline involves four basic questions, all
of which concern the question of security. These are:

1. Is it in the interest of the West to develop the
USSR's energy resources? Opponents of the pipeline argue
that the pipeline will strengthen the Soviet industrial
infrastructure, making the USSR a more formidable enemy.
Proponents, on the other hand, argue that it is in the
security interest of the West to encourage diversification of energy supplies, and the Soviet Union will be
a major source of natural gas in the 1990s, providing a
welcome alternative to dependence on OPEC oil.

2. Is it in the West's interest to increase Soviet
hard currency earnings by paying for natural gas

imports? Pipeline opponents say that the USSR will use
these hard currency earnings to purchase more Western
technology and build its economy and military sector,
forcing the West to spend more on defense. Proponents
counter that these Soviet hard currency earnings will be
more than balanced by the gains to Western economies
from pipeline-related exports.

3. Should Europe double its dependence on Soviet
gas? Pipeline opponents claim that the USSR will use
this European dependence to influence West European
policies. Proponents claim that the USSR is a reliable
supplier and would not use gas exports as a form of
leverage, because it would thereby jeopardize its future
access to hard currency earnings and to spare parts for
the pipeline.

4. Should the USSR receive subsidized credits? The
US firmly believes that the European taxpayer should not
subsidize credits to the Soviet Union. Most European
governments (with the exception of the Germans) argue
that without subsidies, their exports would not be
competitive.

All these issues will continue to trouble the
Western alliance, despite the removal of the US pipeline
sanctions. This is because they involve basic differences over the economics and politics of East-West
trade.

Linkage -- should economic relations be politicized?*
Underlying these divergent interpretations of the
economic and security impact of East-West trade is a
transatlantic debate on the surrounding political
framework. There is disagreement on the extent to which
East-West trade should be politicized. From the American
perspective, which views relations with Moscow on global
terms, détente is moribund if not dead. The Soviets have
violated the rules of the game in Angola, Afghanistan,
the Horn of Africa and Central America, and they have
continued their conventional and nuclear military
build-up. By contrast, the Europeans have always had
more limited, regional expectations of détente. From
their perspective, the USSR has observed its commitments
in Europe, even though it may have violated an American
defined code of conduct in the Third World.
These differing evaluations of détente are reflected
in contrasting approaches to the politics of East-West

*Parts of this section are based on Ellen L. Frost and
Angela E. Stent, "NATO's Trouble with East-West trade."
International Security (Cambridge, MA) Vol. 8, No. 1,
1983, pp. 179-200.

trade. Since the Bolshevik Revolution, capitalist states have assumed that the Soviet Union's economic problems would induce Moscow to make political concessions in return for trade. At various times, the West has used two main forms of trade leverage in the attempt to elicit political concessions: negative and positive linkage. Negative linkage or trade denial uses the stick retroactively as opposed to the carrot. It cuts off trade to punish the USSR without necessarily demanding specific political quid pro quos. Positive linkage, on the other hand, uses trade incentives to induce Soviet political concessions. The promise of trade is often linked to specific political trade-offs.

A trade carrot is also a potential stick -- communication to the Soviets that if they renege on an agreement, the carrot may be withdrawn. Broadly speaking, positive linkage tied to explicit concessions in advance should therefore be more productive than negative or reactive linkage. But this view has historically been resisted by the United States, which has never viewed East-West non-agricultural trade as normal, mutually beneficial economic activity.

There is no evidence that negative linkage -- particularly trade sanctions or embargoes -- has ever changed Soviet policies on any issues that the Kremlin perceives as vital to Soviet national security, be it in foreign policy or on such domestic issues as the treatment of political dissidents. For example, the Afghanistan sanctions -- in particular the grain embargo -- imposed economic hardship on the USSR, but had little demonstrable effect on Soviet external behavior. It is theoretically possible that sanctions are effective as a deterrent. There is no evidence, however, that the Soviet Union will make significant political concessions -- or refrain from pursuing major foreign policy interests -- if the West denies it goods that contribute only a limited amount to its economic development. Quite simply, the means and the ends are totally disproportionate.

Positive linkage, on the other hand, has sometimes worked, but only if the means and ends are commensurate and the trade-offs demanded are realistic. In areas that are more marginal to the Soviet system, particularly humanitarian questions, the USSR in the past decade has responded to positive linkage strategies. In particular, it has allowed some national minorities -- largely Jews and ethnic Germans -- to emigrate in return for economic benefits.

Whatever one's evaluation of political/economic linkages, it is undeniable that East-West trade is a highly political activity. It cannot be depoliticized, nor should it be, because it is one of the West's few available bargaining chips in dealing with the USSR.

Indeed, sometimes the West needs to utilize these levers for symbolic purposes, even if their ability to affect Soviet behavior is limited. However, economic leverage can only be productive if it is carefully exercised, and only carrots work. Joint allied policy is preferable to unilateral US moves. On the other hand, it is naive to believe that East-West trade necessarily leads to more peaceful political relations -- the historial record shows quite the contrary.

Is there any possibility of moving East-West trade from a West-West back to an East-East issue, which it rightly should be? The only way out of the current impasse would be a renewed and vigorous allied search for a new consensus. Firstly, the NATO alliance should attempt to come up with a common definition of security, although this would involve concessions on both sides. Secondly, having agreed that some aspects of East-West trade can be used for political purposes, the allies should work out a graduated series of responses to Soviet actions and use economic levers carefully. These two steps would go a long way to resolving our current problems.

If East-West trade continues to be a West-West issue, it will contribute to the weakening of the Atlantic alliance and thereby challenge Western security. It would, therefore, be preferable for the US and its allies to attempt to work out a common strategy and place East-West trade on a less divisive basis.

9. Russia and the West at the End of an Era

Robert C. Tucker

The complex topic of this volume, the relationships between the superpowers and Europe, cannot be considered to have been fully explored until an attempt is made to put the relationship between Russia and the West in a broader, if you will, an historical perspective. For the Soviet Union of today -- whether present or absent from the international scene, whether actively involved or hunkering down to one of its isolationist periods -- is clearly an inheritor of Russia and of earlier Soviet regimes; while its contemporary behavior responds to contemporary challenges, studying its past actions helps us focus on the possibilities of its responses and the motivations for its actions.

Thus, we can best approach the task of discussing Russia and the West at the end of an era by recognizing that there are always two endings for "eras" in progress; although strangely intertwined, they are clearly different in character. In the case of the USSR, there is an end phase in the life of Russia and her empire; in the case of the West, we are witnessing the end of an era of Western policy vis-à-vis the USSR, the end of an era marked by a particular type of East-West relations. In this essay, an attempt will be made to try to summarize these intertwined processes of change and to bring their salient differences into focus.

Soviet Russia at the End of an Era

The first of these endings can best be seen in Russia, as we witness the end of the era that was ushered in by the revolution of 1917-1921. This Soviet era seems to be approaching some sort of terminus, a crossroad as it were. For Russia, the change that Stalin wrought, a legacy that his successors have preserved, has created a paradox that determines today the life of the Soviet state and its internal equilibrium. The paradox of contemporary Russia can best be summed up in the phrase: swollen -- spent society. For clearly as a state, especially in its military, policy and diplomatic establishments, the USSR remains, indeed, very strong. As a society, as a culture involving a belief system shared by its citizenry, however, it can best be regarded as spent; in this respect, the Soviet era is played out.

It is worth reiterating that the Soviet regime of today pursues a basically conservative policy behind a smokescreen of revolutionary ideological verbiage, for two basic reasons. First, to cover up the facts that domestically it is a swollen state and a spent society. Second, to cover up the fact that externally in any meaningful sense, it is no longer a force for revolutionary change. And it is no longer such a force, even though, in the continuing competition with the West and with the United States in particular, Moscow -- largely for reasons of opportune convenience -- frequently does ally itself with forces for INTERNATIONAL change and even with revolutionary change. It continues to do so because it is good politics, but also because the West frequently allies itself with the forces AGAINST change, the forces favoring the status quo. There is, consequently, a false appearance of a Soviet Union that in the international and domestic arena stands for the forces of revolution.

The falseness of that appearance is evident from the role of change -- suppressor that Moscow has played -- with military force if necessary -- in the thirty some post-Stalin years. Specifically, this role is most visible in the policies implemented by the Soviet elite to continually restrain and suppress the very forces of change in Eastern Europe that make that region a troublesome and even potentially subversive force. The view that the events occuring in the region might be subversive to Soviet domestic existence, found its proof in the history of Czechoslovakia in 1968 and in Poland in 1980-1982. Although these events pointed toward possible paths of resolving Russia's own internal crisis, Eastern Europe's restive presence in the Soviet empire is a force for Russia's own Europeanization. This Europeanization, however, could be considered to be a resumption of the rerun of modern Russian history, away from the pattern of Stalin and that of old Muscovy. And the hesitation of the present elite of Russia to adopt such a task is understandable, albeit regrettable. Nonetheless, this hesitation is clearly another sign that Russia is today at the crossroads of change.

What has historically been a prerequisite for peaceful transformation and change in Russia, has been the presence of an authoritative national leader-figure, such a person, for example as Alexander II, who acted to initiate FROM ABOVE the reforms that Europeanized Russia to a large extent in the 1860s. But unlike the rule of Alexander II, post-Stalin rule has been generally change-resistant under the leadership of men who were beneficiaries of the Stalin terror and the products of the system installed by Stalin. Although Khrushchev's rule may be considered an exception to this generalization, it is only a partial exception at best, since Khrushchev himself was a beneficiary of the Stalinist system, and -- of course -- he had to retreat on many of his earlier reformist or change-oriented policies.

Hence, as a result of the historical processes of Stalinist development in the USSR, the strange situation in Russia today is that at the summit of power there exists a dwindling group of leaders, some of whom are conscious of the need for reformist change and yet are fearful of the logical consequences of reform should the process of change take on a momentum of its own. Against change, on the other hand, there exists a conservative -- and very powerful -- force of party officialdom around the country, represented by a majority in the CPSU Central Committee. The resulting immobilism can, of course, continue for a time, conceivably for years to come, pending incremental changes within the leadership and developments in the state and society. But very likely, the face of Russia ten years hence will be no longer the one we see now. Two potential paths of change that can be envisioned are:

1. A liberalization of society and state within the existing framework, and evolution in the direction of Eurocommunism, toward limited pluralism. This path is fraught with huge difficulties, in part because of the ethnic heterogeneity of the population, the force of nationalities and the reemergence of non-Soviet nationalism.

2. A move toward a nationalistic-military-authoritarian state that would represent the placement of the Soviet order into a receivership, with or without explicit recognition of the shift.

To observers of the East European and Soviet scene, there seems to be a tendency toward the second of these alternatives in the movement that has taken place in Poland. Under Jaruzelski's and the military's rule, this alternative does offer a modicum of stability. Is the menacing development of the Soviet nuclear forces pointed to Europe a sign of just such a shift? It might be, but in my view more likely, it is intended -- insofar as the motivation for this development is more political than purely military -- to enforce West European acquiescence in the indefinite prolongation of the status quo in Eastern Europe. Put differently, Soviet policies regarding middle-range nuclear missiles are politically aimed at keeping Western Europe in a state of concern about its own safety, unless it accommodates itself to the Soviet-East European situation as it now exists; in the Soviet view, thus, for an indefinite period.

Soviet Change and East-West Relations
    Today it is a supremely important task of Western
political statesmanship to play a constructive part in
facilitating Europeanization in Russia and Eastern
Europe. It is an extremely difficult and demanding
challenge to imaginative and humanistic leadership in
the West as a whole. It is, in fact, the greatest
possible challenge in international relations. Visibly,
the era when the West could be content with a rather
simplistic policy of "containment" and "deterrence" --
if ever, in reality, there was such an era -- is ending
and today a far more complex, more constructive policy
looking toward change in the East is urgently needed.
This, of course, does not mean that deterrence can be
neglected, although -- provided that true conventional
parity can be reached -- it could, and in my view
should, be accompanied by a firm declaration by NATO of
a new policy of "no first use" of its nuclear might.
    There are many approaches available to influence the
USSR in the direction of incremental change and the
"re-Europeanization" of its policies, away from the
Stalinist mode. At the risk of simplification, we can
identify two basic and divergent approaches toward
influencing the course of development.

1. The "Hardline" Approach
    This approach, espoused among others by Professor
Richard Pipes, looks to the forcing of change in Soviet
Russia by such a huge buildup in the Western military
might that the Soviet economy will become completely
bogged down due to the Soviet national effort to meet
the West's military challenge. According to the
advocates of this approach, that, in turn, will either
lead to some sort of uprising from below or to the
enforced "marketization" of the Soviet economy with the
expectedly resulting political changes occuring not too
far in the future.
    In my view, this approach seems to be the wrong way
of trying to change Russia. At the very least, such an
approach would strengthen the forces in the USSR working
toward finding a way out of their current impasse
through a military-nationalistic solution and such a
leadership is not likely to be less imperialistic than
that currently in power. Moreover, the adoption of such
an approach would also be highly dangerous because of
its spur to an indefinitely continuing and intensified
arms race and may even lead to ever-greater dangers of
war by accident or miscalculation. Such a policy line,
in my contention, is not the way for Western
statesmanship to go.

2. The "Leadership" Approach
    Directly pitted against the hardline approach, there
exists an alternative, which I loosely label the

"leadership" approach. In contrast to the "hardline" approach, this is not a "softline" method of tackling the Soviets, though those favoring the first appraoch may tend to regard it as soft. It stands for englightened leadership to encourage the forces for healthy change that exist in Russia and Eastern Europe, the forces for ultimate liberalization, the forces for re-Europeanization, themes alluded to in earlier parts of this volume.

This approach starts with the recognition of Western strengths. It is often forgotten that the Western community of states is incomparably stronger, more viable and dynamic than the present Soviet-East European community, above all because it is nonrepressive. In the West the political order does not stand athwart the human need for freedom of expression, for liberty in the non-political, social, economic and cultural spheres of life. Whereas the Soviet Union and the East European states are in deep crisis because their governments are continuously attempting to thwart the natural human tendencies toward greater autonomy of action, greater economic, intellectual and also political freedom, the Western states have few if any such problems. No one is emigrating to the East. No one is seeking to escape from the West. There are no electrified fences to keep the populations of the Western states inside their national boundaries. The movement of people is only the other way: away from the East and toward the West. This is the most eloquent evidence of the strength of the Western society as compared to an East that is strong as a power complex, but desperately weak as a society (excepting such times when the people of the East are under threat of war and nationalistic pride and patriotism are aroused among them).

Thus, the West's problems are not that its societies are unviable, but that these problems, while tractable and soluble, can be most easily solved by unity and coherence. And that coherence and unity frequently seems to be missing among the leaders as they approach problems of security and international policy in the darkening world of the late twentieth century. What should the West do then, what can it do, to encourage Europeanizing change -- if one may express it that way -- in Russia and Eastern Europe?

First of all, it can be strong militarily without being provocative and without seeking to restore a lost military-strategic superiority. While it must seek to be able to mount a conventional deterrent capacity -- regardless of domestic costs to the members of the NATO alliance system -- sufficient to deter a Soviet-WTO attack on the West, the West should be in a strong enough position to be able to adopt a "no-first-use" policy regarding nuclear warfare. By following this course, the West can point out to the East that there now exists a <u>mutual</u> security interest with potent benefits for both sides alike. Thus, both sides have an interest in avoiding a holocaust by not being nervous, not being alarmed and not being fearful that the other side might be on the point of launching a military attack through miscalculation or misperception of the opponent's intentions or actions.

Second, <u>the West must be able to involve Eastern Europe and the USSR in future trade relations</u>. While understanding that the idea of "linkage" does not prevent either side from defending vital national interests, trade integration does create mutual dependencies. Such mutual dependencies, clearly, serve the function of "re-Europeanization" of Russia and the East. As well as offering markets to the West, well-thought-out, consistently defined trade policies also serve the function of showing to the East what it has to lose for violations of mutual norms. Although the European partners of the Western alliance system and the US must sit down together and define more clearly what sort of strategic trade with the East must be prevented -- and here it would be well for many a European trade specialist to look at the broader view, the longer-range view of trade in the pattern of mutual development -- the Europeanization of the East is served most clearly by the integration of Western technologies and processes, and the attending opening up of European ways of thinking in the East.

Thirdly, <u>the West must be able to define its national and regional interests in the Third World far more narrowly than it has tended in the past</u>. Ending the decades-long competition for EVERY country of EVERY movement, just because they "might turn Communist," would serve Western purposes, provided, of course, that in areas well-defined, where we do have interests and allies in the Third World, we do act firmly. Proclaiming an end to a senseless competitiion for dubious "influence" everywhere, by keeping on with this proclamation day in and day out, in all possible councils, and seeing that our message gets through to the deprived Soviet population that does not like to see scarce Russian goods sent abroad, will put pressure on the Soviet government from all corners alike. This approach would also force the USSR to re-evaluate its own "ideological" approach based on the continuous and ever-present "competition between the two systems" and bring benefits to the West in the various forums of international public opinion.

Finally, we must insist on the improvement of human rights everywhere, in the USSR as much as in South Africa. While not basing our relations with any country <u>solely</u> on its human rights record, we must still hope for the improvements of all types of human rights, be they intellectual, economic or political in character in countries considered friendly as well as those not so regarded. Only by holding out the record of the West -- and there is no better record of the observation of human rights anywhere in the West -- can we expect to create enough yearning in the people of the East that will move the unwilling autotocrats in the direction of change desribed by this author: the re-Europeanization of Russia and Eastern Europe.

10. Eastern Europe and the West at the End of an Era

Paul Lendvai

Future developments in Eastern and Southeastern Europe will be determined by the following main factors:

A. <u>Increased contradictions between the tendency of the ruling Soviet power to strengthen its hegemony and the efforts of the client states to gain more independence</u>. These are consequences for as well as causes of political and social tensions in the Soviet bloc. Nationalism and not democratization is the most dangerous challenge to Soviet supremacy, regardless of the fact that striving for national independence cannot be separated from pressuring for increased political freedom. In the eighties the varieties and the intensity of these more or less nationalistic "deviations" will depend partly on the internal situation of the individual states, partly on the particular position or unity of the Soviet leadership, and partly (but only to a lesser degree) on the West's Ostpolitik. To be sure, it would be wrong to view this "nationalization" in the various Soviet-bloc states simply as anti-Soviet tendencies. One must also consider the revival of the partly inherited, partly newly-provoked animosities among the client states that are caused to some extent by the dictated integration efforts. This consideration applies not only to the conflicts between Romania and Hungary, but also to the deeper reasons for Poland's relative isolation within the Soviet bloc.

Nationalism remains the most important centrifugal force which not only weakens Soviet control, but also limits the possibilities for concerted action by the client states and thus indirectly consolidates Soviet supremacy. In this context the indirect effects of the national crisis in Yugoslavia and the volatility of Albanian irredentism should not be underestimated.

B. <u>The worsening of the economic crisis in all countries, without the prospect of any noticeable improvement in the near future</u>. After 35 years of total Communist control, references to the pre-Communist past on the one hand, and to the current misery in the

capitalist West on the other hand, are ignored by the
people as hollow phrases. But the Hungarian reform
experiments must, for reasons of power and political
treaties, remain much more limited than the West
generally assumes. The individual Communist countries
export not solutions but rather their problems
(including poor-quality goods) to their brother
countries. The economic crisis in the West and in the
Third World is an additional factor and, of course, a
welcome pretext for the Party leadership.

C. The succession problem, aggrevated by insecurity
about the stability and unity of the Soviet leadership
under Andropov and his potential, simililarly aged
successors. In this respect Hungary and Bulgaria could
turn out to be weak spots sooner than expected, since
neither Kadar nor Zhivkov will live forever. An
uneasiness about these concrete cases is felt
everywhere, since experience shows that the timely
coincidence of a leadership crisis in a client state and
a continued or still unresolved power struggle in the
Kremlin can suddenly intensify a latent crisis.

D. For the foreseeable future Poland will remain not
only an open sore but also a warning and therefore a
welcome excuse for the Party apparatus to nip radical
reforms in the bud. Also in Hungary there is the
general danger that Party bureaucrats, fearful of losing
their privileges, and the masses worried about losing
their modest standard of living could enter into a
temporary alliance of expediency against the reformers.

E. More than ever since the Communist seizure of
power, the church, and religion in general, have become
a serious danger to the established powers, although to
varying degrees. Poland may be a special case, but no
one can overlook the trend toward a religious upswing in
Slovakia, Hungary and the GDR. The person of the Pope is
an additional factor.

F. The change of generations, in concert with the
above-mentioned points, has become an additional
disintegrating factor. Neither the developments in
Poland nor the growing concern of the leadership in the
GDR, Hungary, and Czechoslovakia about their youth can
be understood in any other way. Rebellion against
hypocrisy, opportunism and dictatorship is growing
steadily among the ranks of young people east of the
Elbe without -- at least up to now -- endangering the
foundations of the system.

G. Finally, one must not overlook the immense
dynamics of the transistor revolution. During the Polish
crisis the whole world was continuously made aware of
the significance of Western radio broadcasts. Fear of
free news is at the same time fear of one's own
credibility and legitimacy. Ideology cannot gloss over
the gap between reality and the vision of
"future-oriented" systems. Ideology -- in this case the

postulate of one single and exclusive truth in politics
which can only be interpreted by the true guardians of
the Marxist-Leninist faith -- remains the indispensible
basis of the monopoly of power and at the same time is
that which distinguishes Soviet-style Communist systems
from modern dictatorships. Nevertheless, future economic
and political development, as well as lifestyle and
living standard, will be determined by multiplicity
rather than by uniformity.

H. A last remark: the element of surprise has
repeatedly disproved prognoses about Eastern and
Southeastern Europe and has swept away rational
considerations. The unthinkable has frequently become
the thinkable, and therefore it is entirely possible
that my rather pessimistic assessments will be refuted
by the facts.

About the Contributors

GEORGE SCHOPFLIN is professor of political science at the London School of Economics where he specializes in the politics of Eastern Europe and comparative politics. He is the author or editor of several books on Communist politics. He is currently working on a textbook on Eastern Europe.

WILLIAM SAFRAN, who holds a Ph.D. from Columbia University (1964), has taught at C.U.N.Y. (1960-65) and has been at the University of Colorado at Boulder since 1965. He has done research and lectured in France, Germany, and Israel; he has written four books (on French and German politics), and has authored numerous book chapters, articles, and reviews on various aspects of Western European and comparative politics.

WOLFRAM F. HANRIEDER is professor of political science at the University of California, Santa Barbara. He has published extensively in the area of German foreign policy, the Atlantic alliance, and the theory of international politics and comparative foreign policy. His most recent book is Fragmente der Macht (Munich: Piper, 1981).

VERNON V. ASPATURIAN is Evan Pugh Professor of Political Science and director of the Slavic and Soviet Area Studies Center at Pennsylvania State University. He is the author of Process and Power in Soviet Foreign Policy, The Soviet Union in the World Communist System, The Union Republics in Soviet Diplomacy, and coauthor of Foreign Policy in World Politics and Modern Political Systems: Europe. He also has published in scholarly periodicals and books.

TROND GILBERG is professor of political science at Pennsylvania State University. He is the author of Modernization in Romania Since World War II (New York: Praeger, 1974) and The Soviet Communist Party and Scandinavian Communism: The Norwegian Case, and has written on Eastern European politics in scholarly periodicals and books.

IVAN VOLGYES is professor of political science at the University of Nebraska. He is the author or editor of more than 20 volumes and a large number of articles on Eastern Europe and the Soviet Union. His latest book, Politics of Eastern Europe, is published by Dorsey Press.

J. MICHAEL MONTIAS is professor of economics at Yale University. He is the author of Central Planning in Poland, Economic Development in Communist Romania, and coeditor (with P. Marer) of East-European Integration and East-West Trade. Professor Montias is also editor of Journal of Comparative Economics.

ANGELA E. STENT is associate professor in the Department of Government at Georgetown University, and a Faculty Associate at its Center for Strategic and International Studies. She has published widely on Soviet relations with Western Europe and on the political aspects of East-West trade. She is the author of the book Wandel Durch Handel? (1983) and has served as a consultant to the Congressional Office of Technology Assessment.

ROBERT C. TUCKER is professor of politics and IBM Professor of International Studies at Princeton University. He is the author of The Soviet Political Mind, Stalin as Revolutionary, Politics as Leadership, The Marxian Revolutionary Idea, Philosophy and Myth in Karl Marx, and editor of The Marx-Engels Reader, The Lenin Anthology, and Stalinism: Essays in Historical Interpretation.

PAUL LENDVAI is professor of politics at the University of Vienna and the head of the East European Bureau of the Austrian Television Network. He also is the editor of Europäische Rundschau and the author of several volumes on East European politics. His latest book on East European censorship entitled The Bureaucracy of Truth was published by Westview Press.

Index